A JOURNEY OF RICHES

Live Your Passion

11 Stories for Living a Fulfilling Life

A Journey of Riches – Live Your Passion

11 Stories for Living a Fulfilling Life

Published by Motion Media International
Editors: Daniel Decillis, Eric Wyman, Yasmin Phillip, Olivia Jayden, and Katie Beck.
Cover Design: Motion Media International
Typesetting & Assembly: Motion Media International

Printing: Amazon and Ingram Sparks
Creator: John Spender - Primary Author
Title: *A Journey of Riches – Live Your Passion*
ISBN Digital: 978-1-925919-57-8
ISBN Print: 978-1-925919-58-5
Subjects: Motivation, Inspiration

ACKNOWLEDGMENTS

———◦◦◦———

Reading and writing are gifts that very few give to themselves. It is such a powerful way to reflect and gain closure from the past; reading and writing are therapeutic processes. The experience raises one's self-esteem, confidence, and awareness of self.

I learned this when I collated the first book in the *A Journey of Riches* series, which now includes thirty-two books with over 300 co-authors from over forty countries. Writing about your personal experiences is difficult, and I honor and respect every author who has collaborated in the series.

For many authors, English is their second language, a significant achievement. In creating this anthology of short stories, I have been touched by the generosity, gratitude, and shared energy this experience has given everyone.

The inspiration for *A Journey of Riches, Live Your Passion* was born from my desire to share insights about living a meaningful and fulfilling life. Each chapter is written by a different author sharing their wisdom on finding their passion for creating a better life aligned with their purpose.

I want to thank all the authors for entrusting me with their unique memories, encounters, and wisdom. Thank you for sharing and opening the door to your soul so others may learn from your experience. I trust the readers will gain confidence from your successes and wisdom from your failures.

I also want to thank my family. I know you are proud of me, seeing how far I have come from that ten-year-old boy learning to read and write at a basic level. So big shout out to my Mom, Robert, Dad, and Merril; my brother Adam and his daughter Krystal; my

Acknowledgments

sister Hollie and her partner Brian; my nephew Charlie and niece, Heidi; thank you for your support. Also, kudos to my grandparents, Gran, and Pop, who are alive and well, and Ma and Pa, who now rest in peace. They accept me just as I am with all my travels and adventures worldwide.

Thanks to the team at Motion Media International; you have done an excellent job editing and collating this book. It was a pleasure working with you on this successful project, and I thank you for your patience in dealing with the changes and adjustments along the way.

Thank you, the reader, for having the courage to look at your life and how you can improve your future in a fast and rapidly changing world.

Again, thank you to my co-authors: Julie Blouin, Victoria Finch, Holly Fair, Debbie McKenzie, Anthony Dierickx, Annette Korolenko, Inarra Aryane Griffyn, Brandon Bates, Patrick Richard Garcia, and Anne Henning.

With gratitude,
John Spender

Praise For *A Journey of Riches* Book Series

———⊸o≪⁄⁄≫o⊶———

"The *A Journey of Riches* book series is a great collection of inspiring short stories that will leave you wanting more!"
~ Alex Hoffmann, Network Marketing Guru.

"If you are looking for an inspiring read to get you through any change, this is it! This book comprises many gripping perspectives from a collection of successful international authors with a tone of wisdom to share."
~ Theera Phetmalaigul, Entrepreneur/Investor.

"*A Journey of Riches* is an empowering series that implements two simple words in overcoming life's struggles.

By diving into the meaning of the words 'problem' and 'challenge,' you will be motivated to believe in the triumph of perseverance. With many different authors from all around the world coming together to share various stories of life's trials, you will find yourself drenched in encouragement to push through even the darkest of battles. The stories are heartfelt personal shares of moving through and transforming challenges into rich life experiences.

The book will move, touch, and inspire your spirit to face and overcome life's adversities. It is a truly inspirational read. Thank you for being the kind, open soul you are, John!"
~ Casey Plouffe, Seven Figure Network Marketer.

"A must-read for anyone facing major changes or challenges in life right now. This book will give you the courage to overcome any struggle with confidence, grace, and ease."
~ Jo-Anne Irwin, Transformational Coach and Best-Selling Author.

"I have enjoyed the *Journey of Riches* book series. Each person's story is written from the heart, and everyone's journey is different. However, we all have a story to tell, and John Spender does an amazing job of finding authors and combining their stories into uplifting books."
~ Liz Misner Palmer, Foreign Service Officer.

"A timely read as I'm facing a few challenges right now. I like the various insights from the different authors. This book will inspire you to move through any challenge or change you are experiencing."
~ David Ostrand, Business Owner.

"I've known John Spender for a while now, and I was blessed with an opportunity to be in book four in the series. I know that you will enjoy this new journey, like the rest of the books in the series. The collection of stories will assist you with making changes, dealing with challenges, and seeing that transformation is possible for your life."
~ Charlie O'Shea, Entrepreneur.

"*A Journey of Riches* series will draw you in and help you dig deep into your soul. These authors have unbelievable life stories of purpose inside of them. John Spender is dedicated to bringing peace, love, and adventure to the world of his readers! Dive into this series, and you will be transformed!"
~ Jeana Matichak, Author of *Finding Peace*.

"Awesome! Truly inspirational! It is amazing what the human spirit can achieve and overcome! Highly recommended!"
~ Fabrice Beliard, Australian Business Coach, and Best-Selling Author.

"*A Journey of Riches* Series is a must-read. It is an empowering collection of inspirational and moving stories full of courage, strength, and heart. Bringing peace and awareness to those lucky enough to read to assist and inspire them on their life journey."
~ Gemma Castiglia, Avalon Healing, Best Selling Author.

"The *A Journey of Riches* book series is an inspirational collection of books that will empower you to take on any challenge or change in life."
~ Kay Newton, Midlife Stress Buster, and Best-Selling Author.

"*A Journey of Riches* book series is an inspiring collection of stories, sharing many different ideas and perspectives on how to overcome challenges, deal with change and make empowering choices in your life. Open the book anywhere and let your mood choose where you need to read. Buy one of the books today; you'll be glad that you did!"
~ Trish Rock, Modern Day Intuitive, Best-Selling Author, Speaker, Psychic & Holistic Coach.

"*A Journey of Riches* is another inspiring read. The authors are from all over the world, and each has a unique perspective to share that will have you thinking differently about your current circumstances in life. An insightful read!"
~ Alexandria Calamel, Success Coach and Best-Selling Author.

"The *A Journey of Riches* book series is a collection of real-life stories, which are truly inspiring and give you the confidence that no matter what you are dealing with in your life, there is a light at the end of the tunnel and a very bright one at that. Totally empowering!"
~ John Abbott, Freedom Entrepreneur.

"An amazing collection of true stories from individuals who have overcome great changes, and who have transformed their lives and used their experience to uplift, inspire and support others."
~ Carol Williams, Author, Speaker & Coach.

"You can empower yourself from the power within this book that can help awaken the sleeping giant within you. John has a purpose in life to bring inspiring people together to share their wisdom for the benefit of all who venture deep into this book series. If you are looking for inspiration to be someone special, this book can be your guide."
~ Bill Bilwani, Renowned Melbourne Restaurateur.

"In the *A Journey of Riches* series, you will catch the impulse to step up, reconsider and settle for only the very best for yourself and those around you. Penned from the heart and with an unflinching drive to make a difference for the good of all, *A Journey of Riches* series is a must-read."
~ Steve Coleman, author of *Decisions, Decisions! How to Make the Right One Every Time.*

"Do you want to be on top of your game? *A Journey of Riches* is a must-read with breakthrough insights that will help you do just that!"
~ Christopher Chen, Entrepreneur.

"In *A Journey of Riches*, you will find the insight, resources, and tools you need to transform your life. By reading the author's stories, you, too, can be inspired to achieve your greatest accomplishments and what is truly possible for you. Reading this book activates your true potential for transforming your life way beyond what you think is possible. Read it and learn how you, too, can have a magical life."
~ Elaine Mc Guinness, Best Selling Author of *Unleash Your Authentic Self!*

"If you are looking for an inspiring read, look no further than the *A Journey of Riches* book series. The books are an inspiring collection of short stories that will encourage you to embrace life even more. I highly recommend you read one of the books today!"
~ Kara Dono, Doula, Healer, and Best-Selling Author.

"*A Journey of Riches* series is a must-read for anyone seeking to enrich their own lives and gain wisdom through the wonderful stories of personal empowerment & triumphs over life's challenges. I've given several copies to my family, friends, and clients to inspire and support them to step into their greatness. I highly recommend that you read these books, savoring the many aha's and tools you will discover inside."
~ Michele Cempaka, Hypnotherapist, Shaman, Transformational Coach & Reiki Master.

"If you are looking for an inspirational read, look no further than the *A Journey of Riches* book series. The books are an inspiring and educational collection of short stories from the author's soul that will encourage you to embrace life even more. I've even given them to my clients, too, so that their journeys inspire them in life for wealth, health, and everything else in between. I recommend you make it a priority to read one of the books today!"
~ Goro Gupta, Chief Education Officer, Mortgage Terminator, Property Mentor.

"The *A Journey of Riches* book series is filled with real-life short stories of heartfelt tribulations turned into uplifting self-transformation by the power of the human spirit to overcome adversity. The journeys captured in these books will encourage you to embrace life in a whole new way. I highly recommend reading this inspiring anthology series."
~ Chris Drabenstott, Best Selling Author and Editor.

"There is so much motivational power in the *A Journey of Riches* series!! Each book is a compilation of inspiring, real-life stories by several different authors, which makes the journey feel more relatable and success more attainable. If you are looking for something to move you forward, you'll find it in one (or all) of these books."
~ Cary MacArthur, Personal Empowerment Coach.

"I've been fortunate to write with John Spender, and now, I call him a friend. *A Journey of Riches* book series features real stories that have inspired me and will inspire you. John has a passion for finding amazing people from all over the world, giving the series a global perspective on relevant subject matters."
~ Mike Campbell, Fat Guy Diary, LLC.

"The *A Journey of Riches* series is the reflection of beautiful souls who have discovered the fire within. Each story takes you inside the truth of what truly matters in life. While reading these stories,

my heart space expanded to understand that our most significant contribution in this lifetime is to give and receive love. May you also feel inspired as you read this book."
~ Katie Neubaum, Author of *Transformation Calling.*

"*A Journey of Riches* is an inspiring testament that love and gratitude are the secret ingredients to living a happy and fulfilling life. This series is sure to inspire and bless your life in a big way. Truly an inspirational read that is written and created by real people, sharing real-life stories about the power and courage of the human spirit."
~ Jen Valadez, Emotional Intuitive and Best-Selling Author.

TABLE OF CONTENTS

PREFACE

I collated this book and chose authors from around the world to share their experiences about what "Live Your Passion" meant to them. The eclectic collection of chapters encompasses many different writing styles and perspectives that embrace the intelligence of our hearts and intuition.

Like all of us, each author has a unique story and insight to share with you. One or more authors might have lived through an experience like one in your life. Their words could be just what you need to read to help you through your challenges and motivate you to continue your chosen path.

Storytelling has been how humankind has communicated ideas and learning throughout our civilization. While we have become more sophisticated with technology and life in the modern world is now more convenient, there is still much discontent and dissatisfaction. Many people have also moved away from reading books and are missing valuable information that can help them move forward with a positive outlook. Moving toward the tasks or dreams that scare us breeds confidence in growing towards becoming better versions of ourselves.

I think it is essential to turn off the television, slow down, read, reflect, and take the time to appreciate everything you have in life. Start with an anthology book as they offer a cornucopia of viewpoints relating to a particular theme. Here, it's fear and how others have dealt with it. We feel stuck in life or have challenges in a particular area because we see the problem through the same lens that created it. With this compendium and all the books in the *A Journey of Riches* series, you have many writing styles and perspectives that will help you think and see your challenges differently, motivating you to elevate your circumstances.

Preface

Anthology books are also great because you can start from any chapter and gain valuable insight or a nugget of wisdom without the feeling that you have missed something from the earlier episodes.

I love reading many personal development books because learning and personal growth are vital. If you are not learning and growing, you're staying the same. Everything in the universe is growing, expanding, and changing. If we are not open to different ideas and ways to think and be, then even the most skilled and educated among us can become close-minded.

This book series aims to open you up to diverse ways of perceiving your reality. It encourages and gives you many avenues of thinking about the same subject. I wish for you to feel empowered to make a decision that will best suit you in moving forward with your life. As Albert Einstein said, **"We cannot solve problems with the same level of thinking that created them." So,** with Einstein's words in mind, let your mood pick a chapter, or read from the beginning to the end and be guided to find the answers you seek.

If you feel inspired, we would love an honest review on Amazon. This will help create awareness around this fantastic series of books.

With gratitude,
John Spender

"Follow your passion, live the life you've imagined, and do what scares you."

~ Christina Koch

CHAPTER ONE

---∽◦◯〜◯◦∽---

Embracing The Love of Life: The Key to Living a Life with Passion

By Julie Blouin

*"There is no passion to be found playing small -
in settling for a life that is less than the one you are
capable of living."*
~ Nelson Mandela

S itting comfortably on the second level of a hilltop home with an open patio door, the warm sun shines through, creating a radiant sun-kissed glow on my skin. A gentle breeze gracefully tousles my long hair, and I feel the soft curls sway away from my face in the wind. As the tresses of hair dance in the wind, they tenderly brush against my shoulders and back, refreshing my skin. It feels like an angel is by my side, supporting me while I pour my heart out in the notebook before me. At that moment, a sense of happiness, serenity, and tranquility fills the room, making this the perfect place to pen this chapter.

As I write, I'm captivated by the breathtaking view of the ocean and the natural splendor of the tall, slender trunks of palm trees reaching towards the sky with their leaves stretching out like a fan embellishing the crystal blue water of the pool. Listening to the exotic birds sing, my heart expands with appreciation. A wave of thankfulness washes over me. I keep reminding myself of my progress to reach this point. I'm so proud of believing in my skills and abilities to succeed.

I'm reminiscing on the power of letting go of what no longer serves my highest potential to make space for abundance to flow into my life. Reflecting on life's highs and lows and the unexpected twists and turns, I am grateful for all the happy and heart-wrenching experiences. Despite pandemic obstacles, I found inner strength, courage, and determination to detach from my old life in Canada and embrace my passions abroad. I listened to the whispers of my heart, took the courage to step outside my comfort zone, and boarded a flight to Costa Rica.

As a life coach, many people struggle unnecessarily to pursue happiness. These struggles often arise because people lack the understanding of simple concepts that can help them live their best lives. They are often trapped in a cycle of negative thoughts, patterns, and beliefs. They are unhappy with their current situation, whether their relationships, career, health, or overall sense of purpose in life. They feel stuck and unsure what steps to take to change their lives.

Everyone has a unique purpose in life, and it is our responsibility to explore and embrace it with all our hearts. I lead by example and show my clients that dreams can become a reality when you have a fearless determination to succeed. I'm motivated to write this chapter to help many people reach their full potential and live their dreams.

This chapter will cover the essence of living with passion and explore five key strategies to support your pursuit of a meaningful life with a clear purpose. Drawing from my experiences and background as a life coach, this chapter aims to inspire and guide you on your path to personal growth.

1. What is passion?

"Passion is the fuel that drives the engine of success."
~ Brian Tracy

Passion is the excitement that steers you toward what you love doing. The more you follow your heart's calling, the more it brings you a sense of accomplishment and fulfillment, regardless of temporary setbacks. When you're passionate about something, you don't give up. Instead, you keep moving forward despite the obstacles. You're determined to succeed and don't easily let anyone or anything get in the way of reaching your goals.

In my life coaching career, when I ask clients what they are passionate about, most individuals don't have an answer to that question because they believe their main goal is to earn a living to support themselves and their loved ones. They can quickly identify what they don't enjoy about their life, but most have never taken the time to silence their mind and look within their heart for the answer.

Most have never truly done deep soul-searching because they are too busy managing their everyday life. They could be spending their time running from one task to the next. As a result, they may feel depleted or not have the time to live their dream life. Although some may believe that pursuing their passion is unattainable, following your passion is powerful. There is always a magnetic pull guiding us to follow our hearts. Ignoring what you love to do can result in feeling like you are fighting against the natural flow of life, leading to exhaustion.

I remember shortly after graduating from university, unable to find employment in my field of study, I took on a soul-numbing job as a full-time data entry clerk in a private company. Thankfully, I only stayed in that position for a few months; continuously doing a repetitive job that doesn't stimulate your mind, creativity, or passions in life can steer you on a self-destructive path. Boring and repetitive gestures become tedious, and a sense of emptiness can creep in, leading to a lack of motivation and feeling trapped in a dead-end job. Life is too short to stay stuck in a career that doesn't ignite the spark within your being.

In my experience as a life coach, people often try to find coping mechanisms to numb their pain from an unfulfilling job by tuning out the whispers of their hearts and turning to alcohol, drugs, or prescription medication. Weekends become a ritual of escape from a life they don't enjoy living. Unfortunately, it's not a solution but rather a temporary break from reality, ultimately leading to more problems in the long run.

Recognizing the importance of finding a meaningful career that would bring me joy, and a sense of purpose, I consciously decided to keep a business mindset and avoid a destructive path. As such, I opted to take on a part-time position as an overnight server at a restaurant in Ottawa, Canada's national capital. Instead of partying, I worked late shifts on Friday and Saturday evenings serving food to those out drinking. I noticed the dangers of substance use as an escape. However, my focus remained on earning money rather than recklessly spending it on activities that do not enhance one's life.

Passion is what I crave to infuse into every facet of my life. I would rather stay single than be in a relationship that fails to stimulate my mind, touch my heart, and nourish my soul. Feeling alone and unsupported in a stagnant relationship is not what I desire. Although I have considered settling for less than I truly want, my heart can't move in that direction. My soul yearns for the possibility of achieving my dreams and living a meaningful life. I refuse to give up on fulfilling my deepest desires and aspirations. Too many people give up on their relationships, and I want to find my forever partner. After reflecting on my goals and vision for a relationship, I agree with Juan Pablo Barahona's advice from his Facebook post on December 23, 2022, "Don't engage in any relationship that doesn't resonate with you 100%, just to see if he or she is the one."

"You were born with potential. You were born with goodness and trust. You were born with ideals and dreams. You were born with greatness. You were born with wings. You are not meant for crawling, so don't. You have wings. Learn to use them and fly."
~ Rumi

2. How do we figure out how to live a life with passion?

The easiest way to discover what you are truly passionate about is to revert to childhood memories. As a child, what games did you play? Whom did you want to become? What could you spend hours creating with ease? Likewise, when you're passionate about something, your creativity flows effortlessly—having a clear sense of purpose that aligns with your values and taps into your skills, abilities, and interests.

Healing and life coaching have always been my passions. From a young age, I have been drawn to helping others navigate their challenges and live their best lives. This passion began at age four when I would alleviate my sister's and friend's headaches and stomach aches. Then, at six, I started coaching my Cabbage Patch Kids in my own "School of Life," teaching them techniques to navigate life effectively.

At sixteen, my life took a difficult turn when my brother passed away, and three months later, I moved away from the family home. Grief-stricken and struggling with emotional pain, I discovered coping skills and naturally coached my friends on resilience and the power of gratitude to heal.

As I grew older, my passion for helping others live their best lives expanded. I obtained a Bachelor's Degree in Social Sciences to study psychology and human behavior to understand better the mind and how it shapes and influences our actions and decisions. I am also a Certified Professional Coach and a Reiki Practitioner, utilizing healing and coaching techniques to help clients solve their problems. To me, healing and life coaching are not just a career; it's a calling that brings me great fulfillment. I love helping others unlock their full potential and to live their lives to the fullest.

"Passion is the secret ingredient that makes life worth living."
~ Tony Robbins

To gain clarity on how to live a life with passion, you can ask yourself these questions:

- ➢ What fuels your soul?

- ➢ What are you naturally good at doing without much effort?

- ➢ What brings you a sense of purpose and fulfillment?

- ➢ What makes you happy?

- ➢ What would you do with your life if money wasn't an issue?

- ➢ How can you bring value to others by feeding your passions?

- ➢ What steps can you take to turn your passions into an income-generating business?

Bringing life into this world was the most profound and fulfilling experience I have ever experienced. It's a journey of unconditional love and transformation from the moment you learn about the pregnancy. Having to do it all over again, I would be a stay-at-home mother and home-schooling, but I was in my twenties when my son was born. As a result, I lacked the knowledge and experience I have today. When my son was born, on the outside, it seemed like I had a perfect life. A loving relationship with an attractive and successful man, a healthy and happy son, and living in the dream house we built together. However, placing my passions and dreams aside to continue working a full-time job and solely taking care of the needs of others was draining. I was too busy and didn't take any time to rest.

Self-love and self-care are the foundations of living a life with passion. They are essential to overall well-being and important in maintaining a healthy and fulfilling family life. I needed balance in my life and to take a step back from my career to focus on my family.

Having met my son's father at a modeling event in Montreal, Canada, during the summer months, I no longer had time to participate in activities I enjoyed other than following him, from racing competitions to car shows. As a result, I often felt like the "trophy wife" standing beside the sports cars and awards at events. I would often ask myself, "When did I only become a decorative status symbol?"

I lost touch with who I was at my core. Material objects had become the focus of our lives, but they failed to bring me joy or happiness. My life felt unbalanced, and I no longer knew my interests. Lacking time and energy, I stopped doing all the activities I enjoyed doing.

Finding out what I was passionate about took some deep soul-searching. Then, feeling lost in the daily grind of life, unable to find my path back to my roots of coaching and healing others, I decided to silence the distractions of my mind by sitting in meditation while opening my heart so I could hear the whispers of my soul to recalibrate the direction of my life.

Our inner voice holds the key to understanding what brings meaning to our life. Through self-reflection, I was able to gain clarity on my passions and take inspired action in the direction of reaching my goals and dreams. Although I had been healing and coaching since a young age, I couldn't fully understand my purpose in life until I connected with my heart and remembered my essence.

The key to getting clear answers on our life's direction is limiting our exposure to distractions so we can focus on what we truly love. Because of distractions such as social media, the television, and notifications from our smartphones, many people have difficulty being fully present with another person or even with themselves when alone. They find meditation challenging because of the constant thoughts filling their head, unable to silence their mind.

Most people need the constant stimulation of social media as entertainment because their life has become so dull, repetitive, and boring that they constantly search for happiness and satisfaction outside of themselves. In today's fast-paced world, we are so focused on getting things done that we no longer take the time to notice the beauty of everything surrounding us. As a result, we forget to admire the sunrise, the delicate scent of blooming flowers, the birds singing, or the vibrant rainbow after a thunderstorm.

I don't watch television, but I love to listen to the waves of the Pacific Ocean crashing down while looking at the sunset. Admiring the effortless and fluid motion of the adorable white-faced Capuchin monkeys jumping from tree to tree is fascinating. Listening to the deep-pitch sounds of the Howler monkeys in the Costa Rican jungle is soothing.

> *"Listen to silence. It has so much to say."*
> ~ Rumi

Following our passion takes drive, courage, adaptability, and determination. It's not always the easiest path in life, especially when instant gratification has become the norm where everyone obtains all their needs without much effort, patience, or perseverance. This can lead to a lack of self-discipline or appreciation for things because everything has become easy to obtain with barely any effort.

I had to embrace a new lifestyle shortly after arriving in Central America. "Pura Vida" is not just a saying in Costa Rica that means "Pure Life," but it is a way of life. It was a rite of passage, from living in North America to adapting to a tropical climate. This process helped me cultivate patience and discipline while staying focused on my goals, despite obstacles. I learned to delay gratification, gain an appreciation for the simple things in life and, most importantly, go back to basics.

In this remote location, roads are mostly unpaved, and you must drive slowly, sometimes crossing rivers. Only essential items are sold here, but you can grow your produce or buy from the local farmers' market. There are many mature fruit trees on the land. People invest in local suppliers, and restaurants serve mostly organic food. Dogs are welcome in many places, including restaurants. Yoga and wellness activities are popular, and the community values family, nature, the preservation of wildlife, and renewable energy. "Pura Vida" helped me focus on life's essentials to find happiness, balance and passion within myself.

3. What does it mean to live your life with passion?

"Passion is the wind in your sails that propels you forward in life."
~ Dr. Wayne Dyer

Getting caught in the need to always do more to achieve more is easy, but success does not equate to the need to do more constantly. It often comes from balancing everyday life and doing what is passionate and meaningful to us. What fuels our fire? What could we do all day, every day, even if we didn't get paid for it?

Many people chase a job title, more clients, more money, or more awards throughout their careers. Still, you will never find a sense of accomplishment and fulfillment when you are not passionate about your job. A void in your life will always be waiting for you to start living with passion. There is a beautiful quote from Confucius, "Choose a job you love, and you will never have to work a day in your life."

Living with passion means waking up grateful and doing what you love. Choosing a career aligned with your purpose brings daily magical experiences. Passion motivates us to achieve great things and view obstacles as growth opportunities, not distractions from our dreams.

Even when faced with adversity, when we let our heart be the compass for the direction of our life and let passion become our north star, we can keep pushing forward regardless of temporary setbacks. On the other hand, not living a life with passion can lead to pain, depression, and sadness. It can keep anyone trapped in a downward spiral of negativity, eventually leading to a lack of motivation. You may become stuck in stagnant energy, leading to dissatisfaction with your life and a feeling of emptiness.

So, what drove me to go to Central America to take a leap of faith toward fulfillment and purpose? One day I woke up with a strong sense of urgency to make a bold move. I had enough of the negative energy of the people, places, and things I had outgrown, which drained my life force energy, limited my progress and potential to succeed, and made me feel trapped in stagnant energy, preventing me from living my best life. It felt like being stuck in quicksand: the more I struggled, the deeper I sank. The constant effort was exhausting, and I knew that my life would significantly improve by changing my surroundings.

When I landed in Costa Rica, I instantly felt a deep connection with my innermost desires, and my life shifted immediately because I was in alignment with my successful career as a life coach. I realized you could reach your full potential by embracing your passion and purpose. When you are in soul alignment, you feel passionate and alive.

Tonight, as I walked past the mirror to brush my teeth before heading to bed, I glimpsed at my reflection. My gaze lingered on my sparkling eyes full of light and happiness, my long hair flipped to one side with gentle curls cascading past my shoulders in the soft glow of the candlelight. I couldn't help but admire the shape of my body in the simple white tank top I was wearing. I paused momentarily and couldn't help but think, "Wow, I am in beautiful Costa Rica, exactly where I had always dreamed of being. Dreams become a reality when you dare to pursue them."

Having the self-confidence to simply BE whom you are destined to be without the need to be someone else is one of the greatest gifts you can give yourself. It is a true expression of self-love and personal freedom. When you live a purposeful life following your passions and genuinely embody your authentic self, you stop seeking fulfillment outside of yourself. Instead, you realize that your power comes from within.

4. What must we do to live a life with passion?

*Too many of us are not living our dreams because
we are living our fears."*
~ Les Brown

To live a life with passion, we must step away from seeking safety and security instead of happiness and fulfillment. Instead, we need to be vulnerable, let go of the fear of the unknown, and fortify a growth mindset where we understand that setbacks are not failures but learning opportunities.

We need to reframe uncertainty with the excitement of the new. It means stepping outside our comfort zone and taking the first step toward reaching our goals. It's important to push boundaries and believe that we can succeed, regardless of what life throws our way. We need to surrender to the flow of our hearts' calling instead of trying to fight against it. It's crucial to follow our inner voice guiding us on a specific path while embracing life's journey and letting go of the need to control the outcome. We don't need to have every detail figured out. We simply need to take the first step.

What is the alternative to living a life with passion? If we are not living a life with passion, does it mean that we are simply surviving by working a job we don't like to pay the bills, put food on the table, and have a roof over our heads? We are destined to thrive, not simply survive. Maya Angelou said, "*My mission in life is not merely to survive, but to thrive; and to do so with passion, compassion, humor, and style."*

Here are five tips to help you live your life with passion:

1. Have a vision and stay focused on your goals:

> *"You are never too old to set another goal or*
> *dream a new dream."*
> ~ C.S. Lewis

When we set clear goals, we can keep our eyes focused on our vision, even when faced with rejection or an obstacle. It's vital to break down the goals, make them specific, and set a time limit for completing the task. For instance, if you want to write a book, you could set a specific goal of completing the first draft within six months. Another example, you could decide to start eating healthy, go to the gym, and set a goal to tone your body and lose ten pounds within one month. If you want to start a new business, your goal could be to have a profitable business within three years and increase the revenue by 25% within six months. Breaking down your goal is essential to success.

The key is to keep striving towards reaching those goals and never give up. It's important to set time aside every day to follow your passion. When you focus on your goals, you stay engaged and motivated to keep moving forward. We must never forget what Antoine de Saint-Exupéry said: "A goal without a plan is just a wish."

2. Don't compare yourself to others:

> *"A flower does not think of competing with the flower*
> *next to it. It just blooms."*
> ~ Zen Shin

It's easy to get lost in comparing ourselves to others. Growing up as an identical twin was challenging for me. From sharing everything, including my clothes and birthday, I had no individuality outside the dynamic of being an identical twin. The daily comparison to my sister led to negative self-talk or never feeling good enough. It was exhausting. I spent my teenage years trying to find my true self by changing hairstyles to look different from my twin sister so people would stop comparing us. I even considered getting a butterfly tattoo, symbolizing metamorphosis and transformation, but I eventually decided against putting permanent ink on my skin. Instead, I experimented with piercings by getting a navel and tongue ring, but I finally removed both.

One day, I came across a beautiful quote by Zen Shin: "A flower does not think of competing with the flower next to it. It just blooms." It made me realize that I was looking for change outside of myself instead of doing the inner work to gain self-confidence, let go of self-doubt, understand that everyone has different skills and abilities to succeed in life and remove the limited beliefs holding me back from becoming the best version of myself. Now, I am bold, fearless, unstoppable, and radiating self-confidence.

3. Practice gratitude and positive thinking:

> *"Gratitude is a powerful catalyst for happiness.*
> *It's the spark that lights a fire of joy in your soul."*
> ~ Amy Collette

We must cultivate a positive, abundant, and growth mindset to live passionately. The easiest way to achieve that is through journaling. By staying in the present moment and shifting our awareness to the positive, we can appreciate what we have and flow into our passions.

What we focus on the most expands. This is why it's crucial to add journaling to your morning routine. Start by writing what you're thankful for, and at bedtime, write down all your accomplishments during the day, big or small. The more you celebrate your success, the more it will create momentum to give you the strength and determination to keep moving forward. Then, when the going gets tough, you can re-read your past journal entries to help you remember all the amazing things in your life that have brought you so much love, joy, happiness, abundance, and passion.

In my everyday life, I embody the concept of positive thinking by living in gratitude. When a challenging experience occurs, I immediately reframe the situation and find something positive. This becomes a natural set point when we live with passion.

4. Surround yourself with positive people:

> *"You are the average of the five people you*
> *spend the most time with."*
> Jim Rohn

Surrounding yourself with positive people who inspire you to become the best version of yourself is vital. Some individuals will drain your energy because their primary focus is soaked in negativity and criticism, while others will amplify your energy by focusing on positivity and encouragement. Be vigilant in selecting your inner circle with vibrant, energetic, and happy people who let you shine as your authentic self and encourage you to fulfil your passion. Nurture uplifting relationships, and as Albert Einstein said, "Stay away from negative people. They have a problem for every solution."

5. Take action:

> *"Let yourself be silently drawn by the strange pull of what you*
> *really love. It will not lead you astray."*
> ~ Rumi

To live passionately, we must pursue our dreams boldly and without excuses. We should leave our comfort zone, take calculated risks, and face our fears. Taking the first step towards our goals creates momentum and builds self-confidence, making it easier to face the unknown. Ultimately, we have the power to choose how we want to live.

As Mel Robbins said in her podcast, The Mel Robbins Podcast, "Why don't you just count backwards and see what happens? Like NASA launches a rocket: 5, 4, 3, 2, 1 [...] Interrupting the patterns of thought and behavior that are holding you back and pushing yourself to take action or to think something different is the only way you're going to change and this is a tool that's going to help you to bridge that gap."

Living with passion attracts abundance and empowers us to overcome challenges. When our purpose and heart align, we can achieve anything and reach our full potential. When we look beyond the necessities of survival, we can tap into our innate power, align with our authentic selves, and identify our skills and abilities to design a meaningful life filled with love, joy, happiness, health, and abundance. We need to embrace life with courage to live our life with passion.

Most people live on autopilot, never exploring what truly ignites their souls. Instead, they go to school, get a job for money, and don't prioritize pursuing their passions because they were never taught its value. Bronnie Ware, a nurse who spent years working in palliative care, wrote a book called: *"The Top Five Regrets of the Dying,"* and the number one regret people on their deathbed had: "I wish I'd had the courage to live a life true to myself, not the life others expected of me."

To help you live a life of passion, having a vision and staying focused on your goals is essential. Don't compare yourself to others. Instead, practice gratitude and positive thinking. Surround yourself with positive people and take action.

Living my best life involves embodying the person I am destined to be on a soul level. It means never toning down who I am simply to fit in the dull backdrop of ordinary life. Instead, it's all about choosing a career in soul alignment by helping others reach their highest potential.

We must have the courage to embrace the love of life by living with passion. It may not be the easiest path, but it is the most fulfilling and rewarding experience. It requires courage, patience, perseverance, adaptability, determination, and resilience. Accepting change and taking risks are all part of the road to success.

Everyone is capable of living a life with passion. All you need to do is to get clear on what ignites a fire within and stimulates your mind. Once you have that figured out, move in the direction of your dreams, and never let anyone dim your light. Living with passion is the key to finding true happiness and fulfillment. It makes life worth living.

"The most powerful weapon on earth is the human soul on fire."
~ Ferdinand Foch

"Never underestimate the power of passion."

~ Eve Sawyer

CHAPTER TWO

---◦◦⌒◦◦---

It's Never Too Late to Follow Your Passion - Find the Joy in Life

By Victoria Finch

"Only passions, great passions, can elevate your soul to great things."
~ Denis Diderot

A s a child, I remember looking up at the clouds and pretending I could see "cloud people."

I had quite the imagination. I would imagine these cloud people had extraordinary lives. Perhaps they were doctors, lawyers, firefighters, and architects who built massive homes and structures.

I imagine them living out their days happy with their contributions to others. When my mind wanders in this direction, I picture a gentle summer breeze caressing my face as I smile. Then I would wonder what I would be when I grew up.

I imagined being married with three children and living in a big house with white columns like we often see in the Southern United States flanking the staircase leading to the front door and towering evergreens on either side.

There were rose and peony bushes of various colors sending fresh fragrance through the air and a swing on the front porch.

However, I wasn't sure what I wanted to be; I only knew that I wanted to make a difference in the lives of others and live in a big house. I got that from my parents and grandparents, who were always willing to help others.

As I got older, something happened: I could no longer see the clouds of people. I had completely forgotten about them. Finally, I lost my bearings, and a new companion replaced my imagination.

I didn't notice it at first. I also wasn't aware that I was drifting farther away from what set my soul on fire. My life became more about paying the bills than pursuing my passion. Before I knew it, fear had become my new companion.

Fear can be incredibly limiting, which is why confronting it is important. Whether it's the fear of not being good enough, failure, or success, it is essential to disregard these feelings and move forward with passion. After all, passion is often the driving force behind our greatest accomplishments. No matter what hurdles stand in your way, staying true to your passion will motivate you to remain steadfast in the face of any challenges.

Fear can be powerful; recognizing, understanding, and moving past it can be fulfilling and liberating. Let me tell you how a lady, Kate, overcame her fear. Kate's fascination with graphic design dates to her childhood. She loved everything related to graphic design and art. Kate enjoyed the idea of graphic design so much that she started to teach herself how to create stunning designs. She even dreamed of someday making a living in graphic design. However, Kate had self-doubt and let fear hold her back. Although she could not let go of the thought of becoming a graphic designer, she still could not imagine being good enough to support herself financially as a graphic design artist.

However, one day, Kate left her comfort zone and enrolled in a graphic design certification course. The course wasn't easy for Kate, but she persevered and got her certification. Then, with the confidence of being a certified graphic designer, Kate started to network and apply for jobs in the design industry.

Finding a position was difficult, as Kate often faced rejection or the position was not right. But, determined, she kept applying. During this time, she was also improving her skills. As a result, she was eventually offered a position as a junior graphic designer at a well-known company.

Kate kept up the hard work and showed her value to the team, and she was quickly promoted to senior design artist. She was finally able to live her passion while enjoying life. Eventually, Kate found herself in a community of like-minded individuals equally enthusiastic about graphic design.

Kate's experience inspired her to give back to the community. She started volunteering at the local technical school for underprivileged children, teaching them about graphic design basics and helping them explore the many possibilities in graphic design. She also started a blog about graphic design to help others interested in the field.

Kate is living the life she has always wanted and finds fulfillment daily in doing what she loves while serving the community. Her story inspires us to move toward our passion despite our fear. The journey isn't always an easy one. However, you can turn your passion into reality with diligence, the willingness to take risks and determination.

Living your passion can bring more than professional success; it's about finding personal fulfillment. Far beyond job satisfaction, working on something you're passionate about can provide a sense of purpose and accomplishment that is hard to replicate. Passion is how we nurture our dreams, pursuits, and interests, allowing us to grow. It motivates us to channel our energy into positive outlets, ultimately allowing us to discover hidden talents within ourselves. Living our passion leads to feeling contentment and joy in the small accomplishments we make along the way; it gives us a platform for developing passions or honing existing skills, propelling us forward as we strive for that ultimate sense of fulfillment!

In my own life, I learned to let go of fear. I decided to let my faith triumph over my fear. We can learn a lot from Kate's story. However, it does bring up the question of discovering your passion. For Kate, it was easy because she loved graphic design. For some of us, it is not entirely black and white.

Now comes the big question: How do you find and pursue your passion? First, you must look deep inside yourself to determine your true values. What are the things that bring you joy? What are your talents and strengths? What are the most common topics on which people seek your advice? You must investigate these things to determine what brings you joy and happiness.

Once you have found your passions, it's time to set goals to achieve them. You may need to consider taking a workshop, enrolling in a course, or perhaps starting your own business. Whatever you decide, it is essential to create a clear roadmap.

I heard Earl Nightingale tell a story of a boat that set sail. But it had neither a rudder nor direction. So, unfortunately, there was no way for the ship to reach its destination. So, having a passion without a clear path is much like that. But having a goal will give you direction. And you will have a much better chance of turning your passion into a reality.

It is also important to surround yourself with, as Les Brown calls them, "collaborative achieving driven individuals." Jim Rohn said, "You are the average of the five people you spend the most time with." You can find like-minded people by joining groups in your area or a community with the same interests. Another terrific way to connect with others is by using the power of technology. We can now connect with others in ways that were impossible 35 years ago. Having the right connections will help you feel a sense of community and give you access to networking and other valuable resources.

Now that you have found your passion, you must understand that living it is a journey, not a destination. It is a process. Sometimes, it is an exceedingly long and difficult road. There will be challenges, roadblocks, and detours along the way. However, these can often be great sources of personal growth and development. At times, staying focused and motivated on our goals may be challenging. It is in these times that we must remember our "why." You can overcome almost anything if the "why" is strong enough.

Moreover, we've often heard that there are no overnight successes. For instance, many well-known musical artists spent years honing and practicing their art. They often perform in small venues for many years, planning their big breakthrough. Therefore, creating a plan to achieve your goal or pursue your passion can create a life filled with purpose and meaning.

Another important aspect of living your passion is learning that you have value and your talents matter. However, so often, we doubt ourselves and our abilities. Yet, we are all unique and special. We have stories the world needs to hear to be inspired. Songs to be sung that give meaning to life. Books to motivate others. We are all change agents. We all matter and have something unique to give to the world. I call it our special sauce.

It is amazing how two people can share the same story, but it is received differently by those listening. One of my favorite bible verses is when Jesus said, "My sheep know my voice, and I know them, and they follow me." John 10:27. You have a story that someone can only hear from you. People are waiting for your gifts and talents. They are valuable.

A client came to me because she wanted to author a book. She knew she had a story that could change lives. But she doubted herself. She said, "I don't believe anyone would care about what I have to say." She was not confident about pursuing her dream of becoming an author. Then I asked her one question: "Who told you what you had to share wasn't important?" She said her mother had told her no one wanted to hear her speak. So many of us carry hurts from others. I specialize in inner child healing, and I was able to help her realize that what she said did matter. She is now a best-selling author. Her book has inspired thousands, if not millions, to change their lives and nurture self-love.

We all have talents distinct from those of others—those uniquely yours to share with the rest of us. Pursuing your passion is vital, as you are equipped with the tools and gifts no one else has—don't let them stay hidden. You were put on this earth for a reason—to make an impact and bring joy through the things that make you unique. It is time to recognize your worth and allow yourself to shine. Your passion can give others who need it a sense of purpose and a feeling of pride. So let your light shine brighter than ever!

Once you know your why, let go of fear, set goals, and recognize your value. Continue growing your mindset. Start to expand upon the knowledge you have. Take personal development courses, workshops, and seminars. Read books that inspire and motivate you to keep going when things get rough.

Now, how do you know if you are living your passion? These seven indicators can assist you in determining whether you are living your passion.

1. You get a sense of satisfaction and that magical feeling of purpose every day. It's exciting to jump out of bed in the morning. You don't need an alarm clock like so many other people.

2. Time seems to fly by. When you are motivated and focused on your passion, you forget how much time has passed. You find yourself in the "zone." You don't take notice of the

passing of time; whenever you're living your passion, it can be hard to track the ticking clock and measure the moments that go by.

3. You have found your purpose. You have clarity, focus, and energy that give direction and value to every aspect of you. Your purpose fuels your passion, enabling you to make meaningful and impactful contributions to others and contribute something useful or valuable to society or the world around you. Although understanding your deeper meaning in life can take on different forms throughout various stages of life, recognizing it offers balance, confidence, restorative energy, and satisfaction so that you can fully live your passion.

4. You begin living for yourself and not others. Living for yourself can be liberating. You rediscover your true motives and ambitions and are no longer inhibited by what others expect from you. The direction of your life empowers you. You feel secure and committed when it comes to your work.

5. You have a deep desire to find a meaningful purpose that extends beyond the bounds of your own life. You crave something special and long-lasting that outlives you. You find yourself striving towards a greater calling. Your passion and purpose create within you a sense of fulfillment beyond just existing in this world. You want to leave a legacy.

6. Your body undergoes physiological changes too. You stand with purpose and power, your head slightly higher than usual. Light radiates from you. Those around you can see that you can genuinely feel yourself coming alive as if courage were bestowed upon you by a supernatural force. You find yourself embodying an action-oriented attitude.

7. You have an unbridled passion for life and its possibilities. You are in love with living. You are perfectly aware of who you are, standing in the power of your hopes, beliefs, and dreams.

If you find your life does not reflect these signs, please don't despair. It is never too late to start making the changes.

Here are some examples of people who followed their passion and became successful later in life.

Colonel Harland Sanders: After dropping out of school in the seventh grade, he followed a winding path of working several jobs that often ended with him quitting in a huff or being fired. But at 40 years old, Sanders decided to try something different by opening his gas station and restaurant next door.

The word quickly spread about this one-of-a-kind spot, and the business started booming!

In 1952 at 62, Colonel Sanders began a new venture, Kentucky Fried Chicken, which would become an iconic American success story.

Julia Childs: She couldn't cook when she graduated from Smith College. She worked in advertising before moving on to government intelligence, where she fell in love with French cuisine. From that moment on, Julia started cooking whenever she could.

Julia was 50 years old when she wrote her first cookbook. Julia was so good that she gained the reputation of being one of the top French chefs in the world. Surprisingly, she became the first woman inducted into the Culinary Institute Hall of Fame.

Ray Kroc: Ray Kroc, a well-known American entrepreneur, entered the fast-food industry in his late 50s with the McDonald brothers. In 1954, they opened the first McDonald's restaurant, which quickly became a huge success and laid the groundwork for a global fast-food chain.

Before joining McDonald's, Kroc spent several decades traveling across the country selling paper cups and milkshake machines. This experience helped him develop a keen business sense and sales expertise, which he later used to make the McDonald's brand a household name. In addition, Kroc's innovative approach to franchising and marketing was critical to the company's growth and success, and he is still a powerful figure in the fast-food industry.

The examples above show that pursuing your passion is never too late.

Growing up, I was surrounded by love but never felt it. Instead of feeling beloved and accepted in my home, I constantly strived to please others to confirm my worth. Yet, no matter how hard I attempted to make an impact or draw attention from those around me, the longing remained unchecked, leaving me invisible despite existing within the sightlines of countless loved ones who cared about me deeply but were unable to reach through that wall built with feelings of insignificance.

Due to these feelings of unworthiness, I struggled with depression. Finally, at age 57, I found myself on the side of my bed, not caring if I woke up the following day. I had fallen into the deepest, darkest depression of my life.

I had lost my passion for being and could not see past my depression. I noticed a bottle of pills on my side table. And as if someone else was controlling me, I reached for the pills. I picked them up and slowly twisted off the cap. As I methodically shook the pills in my hand, I had one thought: no one would miss me anyway. As I lifted my hand to my mouth to take the pills, I heard a voice say, "I made you on purpose for a purpose, and this is not it." It was as clear as if someone was sitting beside me. I knew it was from the Divine, whom I call God.

At that moment, I had a revelation: my heart was broken, and if I wanted to find the light again, it needed mending. My mindset shifted completely—no more pills! Instead of feeling like a victim, something inside me told me there was another way; all I needed to do was open my heart for healing. What better purpose than to take this new-found understanding from within myself one step further—not just heal but become The Heart Healer—so that others can experience life with an unafraid love too? My passion for life and faith was renewed.

I am on a mission to heal the world, one heart at a time. I now hold many certifications in the healing arts, including Cognitive Behavior Therapy.

You can read how I became The Heart Healer in '*A Journey of Riches: The Power of Inspiration.*'

As of this writing, I am 61 years old. I am walking in my purpose. I get to wake up every day and make a difference in the lives of others. I am living my passion.

I have three beautiful adult children. I live in a gorgeous 5-bedroom, 3-car garage home surrounded by beautiful red rose bushes throughout the property. I haven't planted peonies yet, but I have plenty of room for them. The columns have been replaced with beautiful stones I could not have imagined. I have discovered that when you are living your passion, the universe gives you much more than you could have ever conceived.

In summary, leaping to pursue your dreams and live your passion is no small task, but it's worth every ounce of determination and grit you have. In living your passion, remember that having an open mind, recognizing what makes you unique, and valuing yourself are key components of a growth mindset. When building towards financial stability or proactively seeking opportunities to live your passion and achieve success, don't be afraid to take some risks—try new things and explore uncharted paths! Most importantly, reward yourself during the journey: celebrate milestones during your hustle and bustle to remain personally fulfilled. All of this leads to lasting happiness in life.

The cloud people have returned.

"Your work is going to fill a large part of your life, and the only way to be truly satisfied is to do what you believe is great work. And the only way to do great work is to love what you do."

~ Steve Jobs

CHAPTER THREE

―⚬◦⟨⟩◦⚬―

Claiming My Crown:
The Transformative Power
of Loss and Love

By Holly Fair

W hen passion sparks in the darkest places, it shines the brightest light. To help you fully understand how monumental living with passion is for me, I'd like to share how my great sorrow led me to reignite a passionate life living as a Queen!

I have always been a person driven by goals and achievement. So, from an early age, I found joy in creating checklists and getting that great serotonin rush from checking off completed tasks. This practice evolved over the years from little things like "Make my bed" and "Feed the dog" to bigger things like "Finish master's degree," "Get married," "Buy a house," and even "Have a baby."

I have felt passionate about many things over the years, off and on my list. Dancing, following my favorite band (Depeche Mode) around the country on several tours, and throwing myself headlong into various crafts, to name a few. When I am passionate, I go all in! So, when I got into scrapbooking, I didn't just have a few supplies. I had thousands of dollars' worth of gear, including 36 pairs of funky-edged scissors – every style Fiskars made. I still have those scissors, and they've been part of several discussions with my husband, Jamie, as things I could "donate…" but I'm holding fast and keeping them. After all, you never know when you need a heart-shaped cutting edge!

Despite some tough seasons, and several passing passions, life clicked along, and I had successfully achieved everything on my beloved list except that last big one – "Have a baby." I had married young, twice, to men who were right for the time but not for the long haul. So, being the "responsible" person, I prided myself on being, I waited until all circumstances were perfect. Finally, all signs pointed "YES" when I was 40, and wow! Things were perfect!

I was the happiest I could ever remember being in my entire life! Then, finally, I discovered that my dream of becoming a mother was coming true! I had done all the "right" things to that point – I had waited for the "right" man to be the father, had gotten married, had completed my graduate studies, pursued a career I enjoyed, and had both a spacious house and a heart full of love to give.

Jamie researched diaper brands, and I started a journal for my LOLA – Little One Long Awaited. In it, I told my baby about all the fabulous things we would do together – how this life is magical and how very loved and wanted she was! I was excited to share my passions for learning, music, travel, and art with my soon-to-arrive baby!

After two short weeks of bliss after the positive pregnancy test, I felt too good; I had an instinct that something was wrong. My doctor ordered an ultrasound, and as I lay on a cold table in a cramped, utilitarian room, I heard the awful words, "I'm so sorry, it's an ectopic pregnancy." My heart sank. I knew the prognosis by the look on the doctor's face. A healthy pregnancy wasn't possible with the fetus growing in my fallopian tube. Those words instantly shattered my future dreams.

I was quickly whisked from the clinic to the hospital, where I again found myself lying in a cold, sterile room. Furthermore, waves of emotions flooded me, but I was mostly numb – this had to be happening to someone else; I felt like I was observing from outside my body. The nurses couldn't even find a vein to start my IV and needed specialized equipment from the NICU to do so. My entire body was resisting this fate, fighting against the upcoming tragedy.

How could this be? Was this all just a horrific nightmare? I was so happy! Then, with the removal of that fallopian tube and the heartbeat I'd heard for only seconds, my life was in shambles – and just two days before Christmas.

The holidays afterward were bleak. My grief was profound. I heard people laughing in my home on Christmas Eve. How dare they laugh when I was dying inside! With rage, I shot out of my bed to give them a tongue lashing and cut them down to the despair I carried. Well-meaning people said things like, "It wasn't meant to be," "It's for the best," "I know exactly how you feel," and "You'll get through it." But I didn't want to have to get through anything – I wanted my baby. Her name was Aurora. I had felt her spirit within me and missed her so.

This tragedy blocked my emotional access to passion and my zest for life. I couldn't imagine ever recovering and positively wallowed in my misery – but I couldn't hide forever. Jamie is part of his company's senior leadership team, and we've been invited to countless events over the years. Three months after my tragic loss, a management planning retreat was held where spouses were invited to stay at the hotel and join the team during meals over two-and-a-half days. I joined those meals with all the courage I could muster, though I hid in my hotel room the rest of the time.

Dinner on that first night was at a luxe Mexican restaurant – my favorite cuisine! It was a place I hadn't eaten before, and I was looking forward to the meal. I did okay throughout the conversations until another couple talked about how much fun their new baby was and how much they missed him while at the retreat. After that, I had to excuse myself before tears swept away the entire group and me. Luckily, the restaurant was next to the hotel, so it was an easy getaway.

The next night's dinner was at a super-upscale steakhouse. As a vegetarian, it was not my favorite type of fare, so I was already on edge – particularly after discovering exactly one item on the menu that I could eat. Then, as the company owner had a tradition of doing, he posed a question for the group to stimulate conversation. His question was, "What's the worst thing you can imagine happening to you?" That question – that horrible, thoughtless, emotion-stirring question both shocked and disempowered me. He, and everyone at the table, already knew about my situation. So why would he tread into such dark waters?

The responses were dreary, and I determined I would not play along this time; I wasn't about to leave again bawling. When it was my turn, I said, "I'll pass." The owner gave me an understanding nod as he finally realized he had just created a nightmarish scenario for me and went on to the next person. She responded, "Losing a child." I gasped, fumbled out of my chair, told Jamie he could stay and eat, and left in tears. It was about a mile walk back to the hotel, and I sobbed the entire way.

Feeling alone, I called my mom and told her of all that had transpired. She listened and gently suggested I avoid the rest of the joint meals and find a therapist to help me through the grief. This advice sounded reasonable, and I awaited Jamie's return to explain it all to him.

My loving husband was embarrassed – his wife couldn't even get through a meal with his colleagues without "making a scene." When he returned to our hotel room, I told him I wouldn't join him for the next day's finale lunch. He pleaded with me to try. "I have been trying! I've tried and tried and just can't try anymore!" I replied. Disappointed, he finally understood and went solo.

When we returned home, I reconnected with a counselor I had seen years ago. She knew my history, and getting her up to speed was easy. She helped me see that what I was experiencing was normal and that it was okay to feel these feelings. Instead of hiding away from them, she said to flow with the waves as they come – to let myself cry when in the grocery store seeing a pregnant woman with three other kids in tow – to let it out and deal with it so it wouldn't compound itself and become worse. Through therapy, I determined I was ready to open my heart to another pregnancy.

Due to my "advancing years," my doctor encouraged me to see a fertility specialist. I cobbled together the strength to see the specialist, and for the next two years, we tried every infertility treatment under the sun – none of which was covered by our insurance, of course. Ovulation-stimulating drugs, hormone therapy, Intrauterine Insemination, acupuncture, energy healing – each month, hating myself and my broken body when my period came.

These feelings of self-loathing propelled me back to a state of worthlessness and nothingness, which had been ingrained in me as a young child through repeated sexual abuse by my grandfather. Part of me felt that if I wasn't good enough to be protected and loved back then, I must not be good enough to create life. I had lost my passion for almost everything.

Throughout this time, I figuratively and literally cocooned myself in bed. I was an online professor with tenure, so I could keep my job with minimal effort, all while wearing pajamas and not brushing my hair. I stopped caring about anything; my body, home, and relationships all showed it. Those hormonal treatments wreaked havoc on my weight, and eating junk while getting no exercise didn't help, either.

I only ever really left the house for obligatory events. And eventually, Jamie had another one of those company parties – this time, a black-tie gala. I was much heavier by now, wearing a circus tent-sized gown. I undoubtedly projected an air of "please don't engage with me. I'm in misery and won't crack a smile." Just as I felt I couldn't be any more miserable or self-conscious, one of the other wives walks with a hefty baby bump.

My vision narrowed, my heart pounded, and the tears flowed uncontrollably. I leaned into Jamie and said, "She's pregnant – AGAIN!" He looked sick and said, "Yeah, I found out earlier and forgot to tell you." "You 'forgot' to tell me? You thought it would be better for me to be surprised at this event?!?" I snapped!

With rage at him for allowing such a sensitive subject to slip his mind and overwhelming sadness, I fled with a speed my feet hadn't seen in years to the bathroom, where I sobbed throughout the meal service. After a while, one of the other wives came in to check on me and said they were worried. Finally, I collected myself and rejoined my husband, who had visible disgust and embarrassment on his face.

No wonder I relegated myself to my bedroom. There, I could control whom I interacted with and what I saw, which was a lot of Netflix and not much else.

I watched the calendar flip each month and heard my biological clock tick-tick-ticking away. Our last hope was In Vitro Fertilization. IVF was the most expensive and intensive of them all. We got the news of IVF failure on Valentine's Day. Not exactly the best timing for a romantic evening. We were left with nothing but crushing news, over $20,000 gone, and a Sharps container full of used syringes. By this time, I was 43, and my biological clock had ceased ticking. I resigned that being a bio-mom wasn't in my cards.

That resignation left me with a heavy heart and many regrets. I did everything right! I was responsible! On paper, I was the best candidate to be a parent! Why me? Why did I wait so long? What's wrong with me? I had lost all passion for life. I felt like I had nothing to live for. It reached the point where it was a victory just to have an occasional shower.

Jamie despaired. He felt as if he'd lost both his baby and his wife. He pleaded with me to "rejoin the living" and be his partner again. I would try for a day or two but then always retreat to my hermit existence again, worrying that I would lose him, too.

One day in one of my Netflix-induced comas, I happened on the Netflix documentary "*I'm Not Your Guru*" – a story about Tony Robbins' six-day Date With Destiny event. A spark of hope glimmered as I sat Jamie down to watch it. By the end of the movie, I knew I had to go. I looked at Jamie and said, "We're going!" With that, we planned and booked our travel and accommodations for the next event.

We attended DWD in December 2018, and, as I had done so often in the past, I threw myself passionately into the event. When the music played, I danced! When we had writing exercises, I poured out my heart! When we watched interventions and listened to the content, I took notes as if my life depended on it – because I knew this was my lifeline!

Suddenly, I had more passion for life and found myself reaching out again to total strangers, telling them that I saw them, acknowledging their greatness, and honoring them for the steps they took to transform their lives. Holy schmoley – I was back! Finally, I felt and engaged the way I had before my loss; seeing it was beautiful!

Near the end of the last day, Tony Robbins had one more exercise for participants to integrate the transformations. Then, I heard MY name called out to join him on stage! Hearing my name was like a song from heaven – I felt the call to greatness in my gut and sped up to the front of the room, all 276 pounds of me, ready for my moment! I can tell you, there's nothing quite like having Tony Robbins' undivided attention to help you gain perspective on how your life will never be the same again monumentally!

When I took the stage, Tony asked me some questions and read my poster that contained my old story, my rules for happiness, and my new story. I won't spoil the particulars of the intervention for those who haven't done it, but it was life-changing. I was in my element and owned that stage like you wouldn't believe!

I played full out in all my shining glory! Over 5,000 people were on their feet, standing on chairs, cheering, crying, and rooting for me as I declared with volume, determination, and triumph, "I AM A QUEEN, "and brought down the house with uproarious elation! I realized I was part of a beautiful, loving world in that glorious moment. Humanity is good. They're all "Team Me," and I'm "Team Them!" Life is happening FOR me, not to me, and I felt alive!

My intervention has since been replayed in the virtual world; by now, tens of thousands of people have seen it. I've had countless individuals contact me, letting me know how much my transformation meant to them – how I inspired them – how thanks to that video, they could get past their insecurities and play at a higher level than they believed was possible. I've also had people ask me if I was a "plant" because I seemed to be too damned good up there. Ha! No, I wasn't a plant. Instead, I saw the opening to the door of my greatness, and I seized it with passion and grace!

Since that seminal moment, I have done thousands of hours of inner work. I've up-leveled my life and truly claimed my Queen identity! I'm not "the" Queen; I'm "a" Queen, one who leaves room for every person on this planet to recognize their inner royalty! As I have developed what a Queen being means, I've come to realize that, for me, a huge part of that is showing up and shining – shining so brightly that I light the way for others and permit them to be just as big, bright, and beautiful, and to live with passion!

I changed my eating habits and joined a posh athletic club. Next, I hired a personal trainer and put my passion and drive into regaining my health and feeling good about my appearance. At first, the weight loss was slow, but I persevered, and eventually, as I shined brighter and showed up for myself, the excess pounds started falling off more easily. Yes, I know, it sounds like some tacky line from an infomercial, but it's true! Loving myself and appreciating my beautiful body's resilience, character, curves, and womanhood led to wondrous results! All in all, I've shed 141 pounds since that intervention! Talk about reigniting my passion for living my best life.

Living my Queen life inspired me to buy a beautiful tiara. At first, I wore it only for Zoom coaching calls and fun travel photo ops. But I received such positive comments that I've worn it daily for nearly a year and a half – shopping at the grocery store, trail running, visiting the dentist's office, and traveling the world. When I wear it, people notice it – it stands out; I stand out! It gives people a reason to look at me, and I respond in kind. I look back at them – in the eye. I flash a warm smile and invite connection and conversation. I see myself as an ambassador for the royalty that lives within us all!

Remember those horrible company events I told you about earlier? I want to regale you with another story about the holiday party in 2022. The suggested attire was an "ugly sweater." I tried many different things and decided on a kitschy "cats in Santa hats" dress – not a sweater, but seriously hitting the desired gaudy theme. I embellished the look with red tights, a frou-frou crinoline skirt, and my tiara. I felt like a million holiday cheer bucks!

The event center was full – well over 120 people. Hors d'oeuvres were passed, drinks were served as employees, and their spouses mingled and commented on each other's chosen holiday outfits. The buffet line opened, and a dueling piano act would shortly take to the stage for entertainment. Knowing I wanted to be up close and personal with the show, I sought out the front, center eight-person table, which was surprisingly sparsely populated with only two others. My husband and I sat down and were joined by two others who wanted in on the action and another person who came solo.

As we ate, the musicians outlined how the evening would unfold. There were little papers on each of our tables, and we wrote our requests and submitted them at the front of the room. As a music lover, I filled out several forms with diverse songs, and others followed suit. The requests rolled in, and the music was belted with humor and talent. I sang along and grooved in my chair until the music swept me away – during the third number of the act!

It was a fun song, and I turned to the lady sitting next to me, singing her heart out, and said, "Wanna dance?" She giggled, and we both stood up and moved to the beat. After that one song, I noticed her glance back at the rest of the ballroom – six tables deep by five across, and no one else dancing but us – and her spark dimmed. Finally, she made an excuse about being tired and returned to her seat.

I wasn't bothered by being the lone dancer. Undaunted, I didn't miss a beat! I permitted myself to freely and authentically express myself through dance and have as much fun as possible right then! Pretty soon, an adorable gal I had just met that night approached and said, "I love your vibe and that you don't care if anybody else is dancing! You're my people, and I want to join your party!" I hugged her and said, "Thanks, you're right, and you're absolutely welcome!"

I danced my heart out for over an hour. I was joyful to dance, sing, celebrate, and move from the heart! At my side was my new friend, and we were joined off and on by a few other ladies whom the dance bug had bitten. By the night's end, the hesitant gal "too tired to dance" had risen to her feet and let herself be moved by the energy.

As we left the party, I was given several compliments and overheard a few conversations. A group of ladies told me I looked like I was having so much fun. When I replied, "The dance floor is open to everybody! Next time, you could join me!" I was rebuffed with, "Oh, I'm too shy," "I'm not brave enough," and "I'm too self-conscious to do that." Finally, I replied, "I've got enough bravery for all of us!"

Jamie's boss said, "We talked about how much energy you have! You danced all night and were the life of the party! You were dancing and having so much fun, but your husband wouldn't get up and dance with you." To that, I playfully replied, "I don't need a man to dance." He instantly blushed and backpedaled.

Back home, I beamed with delight, telling my mother-in-law about the night as I described how much fun I had. Then, as I spoke with her, I relived all that joy again. I couldn't wait to write about it for this very chapter!

A major insight I gleaned was this: Dance like everybody's watching you . . . because they are. How you show up permits them to show up in a gloriously passionate way for themselves!

Observing others is human nature, which has served our species well by keeping us alive. Of course, we make instant assessments of people to determine our levels of safety. But, knowing that the world is watching, wouldn't you rather be seen in a positive light? Isn't it nicer to be seen as the life of the party, the joy maker, or whatever your flavor of passion is?

Now, I'm not suggesting you "fake it 'til you make it;" that's passé and doesn't work because it's faking something that's not you. The key to this approach working is finding YOUR passion – your real, authentic, genuine, full-fledged unapologetic passion – living it and expressing it! Living a juicy passion-filled life is about letting go of the need to fit in. It's about embracing all your quirks and charms and opening your heart, allowing the world to see the joy that is YOU!

Think about how someone radiates when talking about what they love. Their eyes light up, and their tone brightens; their gestures become bigger – they grow and glow right before your eyes. People are attracted to people who are living their passion. We are like moths drawn to the light – we want to bask in the warmth and the glow. Be that passion! Be that light! Love your life!

Passion now fills my soul! I'm living out loud, shining bright, and having fun! This creates joyous moments and a safe space for those around me to do what is truly in their hearts! By permitting ourselves to be authentically us, we can play bigger – smile wider – dance freer.

What I used to call my "life's great sorrow" of losing my baby has now become "My Queendom – the royal gift my angel baby Aurora gave me!" I feel so blessed and grateful for that experience! I am filled with a passion I didn't think possible, and I have lived to be a light in this world!

I challenge you – here and now – to find and express your very own flavor of passion! Be fully engaged in life's beauty. Present in the moment. Present with people. Show up as a beacon of what's possible. Check your self-doubt at the door. Speak and act and love from the heart. Instead of dancing like no one is watching, how about flipping the script and dancing like the world is watching!?! There's always room for you on my dance floor; I'll even help you polish your crown!

"Passion is different from interest. Those who are just interested in things have the "wish," but passionate people have the "will."

~ Israelmore Ayivor

CHAPTER FOUR

⸺∘〰∘⸺

The Bibbulmun Track

By Debbie McKenzie

It all started through a chance meeting. I was taking my routine walk around the lake, and striding towards me was a woman outfitted with a large backpack and hiking poles. I asked her in passing if she was training for the Camino. She noted that she had already walked it twice and was preparing for a thousand-kilometer hike in Western Australia from Perth to Albany, known as the Bibbulmun Track. Upon hearing her response, my heart opened wide in resonance, knowing that she was divinely guided to bring this information as direction for my Bibbulmun mission.

I wouldn't consider myself an experienced hiker by any stretch of the imagination. My longest solo hike of ten days was several decades ago when I was young and fit and quite the contrast to the overweight person I am today. However, my passion was ignited, and I planned my trip by watching video recordings of others who had completed the hike.

It might sound obvious that all the videos would show a glamorized version of people following the yellow brick road to the promised land of unobstructed pathways, gradual gradients, clear skies, and abundant wildlife, and not a trace of the discomforts evident to me from the moment I stepped onto the trail. Nevertheless, I now listen with amusement at a recording I made and sent to my sister overseas after day one, although I was far from amused at the time.

My pack weighed around thirty kilos, double the recommended for a thru-hike. Combine this with the terrain of peaks and valleys

49

negotiated via huge boulders carved into a staircase for giants, one that I would never have been able to reach without my poles. In addition, the valleys were filled with smaller unstable rocks that challenged the toes as they were repeatedly pushed forward to the tips of my boots.

It sounds absurd to have run out of water as I arrived at a Camel Farm five hours into my walk. But, somehow, looking for water at a Camel Farm didn't make sense; perhaps that is why it happened to be closed. Fortunately, the owner was inside, and my presentation, combined with her knowledge of an 8.5-kilometer diversion still ahead of me, prompted her to offer support. Diversions are common on the trail, as planned burn-offs are considered the best way to control fires that can spontaneously occur during the hotter months with devastating consequences.

The owner of the Camel Farm is, as I discovered, a "Track Angel," and these track angels avail themselves to support the hikers in various ways, offering transportation, accommodation, food drop-offs, and a long list of other good deeds dependent on the needs of the hiker and the volition of the track angel. It was clear that I was exhausted when I arrived, and this track angel made me a cup of tea and offered to drive me to the camping ground diversion, which would be my home for the night. As darkness approached, I mustered up just enough energy to erect my bivvy tent, inflate my mattress, and crawl my aching body into its resting place.

The camping ground largely consisted of burned-out trees, and I felt quite vulnerable in my freeway-adjacent tent as a car turned in, pulled up close to my tent, and turned off its motor and lights. I lay there exhausted yet hypervigilant as I tried to ignore the realization that I needed to go to the bathroom without drawing attention to myself by turning on my headlight. Finally, after several hours, I put on my metaphorical hero cape and braved the darkness.

By morning I was dripping wet and assumed it had been raining. However, on closer inspection, the tent outside was bone dry, and the water was all the condensation from my expired air in such a confined space. I was clearly on a steep initiation into a world I was unequipped for. I had no energy and still hadn't eaten since the morning of the previous day when I had filled up on a cooked breakfast. Despite my blistered feet and aching joints, I set off on day two. However, as more giant boulder-like steps came into view, I knew I had to rethink my strategy to see this hike to its completion.

I returned to a caravan and camping site, where I met a couple who drove me back to the hotel I had been staying in. I arranged to have the contents of my pack reviewed by the Bibbulmun Track Foundation as part of their service to hikers. I made the necessary adjustments, including securing a lighter-weight tent that I could at least sit in and a lighter-weight sleeping bag. I reduced the overall weight of my pack by ten kilograms. I saw a podiatrist for a foot and shoe assessment, and I wasn't surprised to hear that many hikers lose their toenails because of the trauma they experience on such a long hike.

> *"As life is action and passion,*
> *It is required of man that he should share*
> *the actions and passion of his time,*
> *at peril of being judged*
> *not to have lived."*
> ### Oliver Wendell Holmes

It might be fitting before resuming my journey to share a little about the Bibbulmun Track, which was named in recognition of the early Indigenous people of the southwest, who were known to walk long distances through the forests for ceremonial gatherings. It was anticipated that the walkers would feel the connection, the reverence, and the oneness of the Bibbulmun People of long ago. Track markers featuring the Rainbow Serpent, known as the Waugal (meaning Spirit), are situated at five-hundred-meter intervals, terrain permitting, to guide the way. Rock towers are evident where placing a track marker, such as at the top of mountains, and leading back onto the trail is more challenging. Many people use Track Apps for these situations. I found myself using my Track App along a beach where I missed the Waugal, which was attached to a tiny post that the surrounding flora had camouflaged. Track Apps work without an internet connection, which is often unavailable except in the towns.

Sparking the Bibbulmun's inception, a passionate soul named Geoff Schafer proposed a long-distance trail after walking the six-hundred-and-fifty-kilometer Victorian Alps and noting no comparable track in Western Australia. Geoff wanted to share his passion for walking so others could access various sections of the trail or complete it end to end. As a result, the track has extended and transformed over the years. After the comparison dismayed Jesse Brampton, a Perth man, it has since been remodeled to resemble the Appalachian Trail. He compiled a detailed proposal to include shelters, adequate water supply, signage, track maintenance, and shifting the trail off gravel roads to the natural landscape.

Many people are passionate about the Bibbulmun trail, and opportunities abound to be involved directly or indirectly in providing support. For example, local prisoners built three-sided shelters in a low-security prison as an initial trial. The success of this project—and the difference it made to the self-esteem of the prisoners, who were passionate about being part of something greater—quickly spread to other low-security prisons, resulting in all forty-nine shelters and water tanks being installed along the entire length of the track. In addition, drop toilets have been donated by individuals passionate about contributing their resources to benefit the hikers.

There are seven towns that hikers pass through on the trail several days apart and allow hikers to rest, have a hot shower, wash clothes, stock up on food, eat a hearty meal, and enjoy the comfort of a hotel room. This makes it a fifty-six-day hike if one stays in each hut and town; however, it doesn't include an additional rest day in the town.

Volunteers maintain the track in seven-kilometer sections, including keeping the track as clear as possible, cutting back overgrowth, and maintaining the track markers, shelters, and guest logbooks that hikers must complete at each shelter to track their journey should they not return in the expected timeframe. The trail attracts over eighty thousand visitors annually, and approximately one hundred people complete the trail from end to end within the same year.

Some people take side trips to explore the geography more thoroughly, while others are in a hurry due to work, visa, or other commitments. Then some like to chase the record for the fastest completion, which currently stands at ten days. If you are curious, the longest record time to complete the end-to-end is twenty-four years. The male-to-female ratio of hikers on the trail has changed from seventy-thirty (male to female) in 2015 to fifty-fifty in 2021.

Many don't have the time to walk the trail end to end, so they will walk a section at a time and complete their hike over several years. Others prefer a day walk or a weekend and enjoy it with their children.

The track has three regions where the terrain changes. The Darling Range in the north from Kalamunda to Balingup includes Jarrah and Marri-forest. The Karri Forest region is between Balingup and Northcliffe. Finally, the South Coastal Forest hinterland, known as the wetlands, is between Northcliffe and Albany.

As magnificently strong and majestic as the trees appear to be in these forests, they are also remarkably delicate. All the internal life exists between three paper-thin layers of tissue beneath the bark, which essentially keeps the tree alive. Trees are incredibly efficient at moving hundreds of gallons of water from their roots to their leaves. They have a sophisticated defense mechanism to protect themselves against organisms threatening their existence. Dieback is a generic term to describe a disease that has occurred along the Bibbulmun track via infested soils transferred through machinery and boots. Boot-cleaning stations have been placed in targeted areas to help prevent the spread of Dieback.

The average distance between shelters is around twenty kilometers, although this varies considerably. Often, the terrain factors into how far the huts are apart. The huts at the north and south ends of the trail are deliberately closer together to give hikers a chance to adjust to the track in either direction of their intended travel.

During the walk, some hikers will reach two huts in one day, known as double hutting. This saves them from carrying as much food and minimizes the weight of their packs. The guest book in each hut follows the journeys of those one might have met earlier on the hike and have moved on. It becomes like a little community.

I bypassed a section due to burn-offs and track diversions. I resumed my journey from Dwellingup, where I met many short-stay walkers walking opposite me, including folk from the Perth Zoo who identified the bird of a feather I was gifted.

I met a local couple who'd embarked on a four-day hike and appreciated the solitude of the shelter after being in the company of thirty others the previous night. Loud snoring is just one of the experiences one quickly learns to adjust to unless a tent site is found far enough away from the shelter to prioritize the healing effects of restful and sound sleep. Fortunately, as reflected in the guest register, I didn't experience the overcrowding that others did.

Meet Feather-foot, a Belgian man who was reclaiming his life after nearly losing it to the experimental vaccines mandated in his country. As a result, Feather-foot could not walk and was bed-bound for eighteen months. Nevertheless, he passionately desired to complete a chapter he had started twenty-four years earlier when he walked a section of the Bibbulmun track. He dreamed of returning one day to walk it end to end.

Feather-foot walked with such a lightness that he seemed to be floating above the ground much of the time. Even during the water-flooded parts of the trail and heavy swamp areas, Feather-foot seemed to tiptoe over the rocks and logs as if they were strategically placed with him in mind. For me, it quickly became clear to walk through the water-logged swampy trail; as much as I tried to emulate his skill in avoiding the water-flooded track areas to keep my feet dry, I would get wedged between tree branches, lose my footing, and prolong the inevitable tumble into the swampy soup.

We walked in companionable silence many days, and his knowledge of the land and its creatures was astounding. He would stop and point to something of interest, give it a name, and continue on his way. This was a welcome departure from my routine of staring firmly at the ground to avoid trip hazards. Without his insights, I would have been oblivious to the tiger snakes, dugites, lizards, varied birdlife, and even the emus, foxes, wild pigs, and kangaroos. On one occasion, I noted the sound of motorbikes in close vicinity. He promptly turned towards me and said, "Motorbike frogs." I thought he must have been joking and expressed my surprise and delight. His knowledge and insight continuously inspired me. He gifted me with a yearling cockatoo feather, which will remind me of the journey and be a beautiful keepsake for my ever-growing feather collection.

Feather-foot continued his journey after I took an extra day to rest, and he completed his end-to-end hike, finishing in Albany. His entry in the visitors' book referred to this experience as a beautiful journey and the closing of a chapter.

Meet Mr. Thirty-Three, a French man who had thirty days' leave from his job as a ranger in a national park and was on the trail to photograph and learn about the various species of orchids. He had calculated that he needed to walk at least thirty-three kilometers daily to complete the hike in his allotted period. He equipped himself with thirty days of dehydrated meals, muesli, and a very heavy camera, and he completed the trail by double hutting all the way. He looked emaciated and exhausted when I met him around the halfway mark of the hike, and one wonders about his condition by the end of the trail. He was flying back to France on his last trek day, arriving just in time to start work. It's all possible through the power of living your passion.

Meet Mattress Man, a forty-something-year-old Perth man who was traveling with another guy who'd incurred an injury. They were taking a rest in one of the towns. As it happened, the injured guy could not complete his hike, and the mattress man caught up with me in one of the shelters as he continued his hike solo. The mattress man had the loudest mattress, which sounded like a jumping castle whenever he shifted positions. So, it was a relief to hear, after my experiencing two sleepless nights, that he decided to double hut. I saw his name in the guest book at the finish line.

I met a twenty-two-year-old German girl who had completed the walk in thirty days, and her pack weighed an impressive six kilograms. With the benefit of hindsight, I would travel much lighter than even the experienced walkers recommend. However, she didn't carry a tent or a stove, and her passion for hiking commenced with the Canary Islands, followed by the entire length of New Zealand, before her adventure on the Bibbulmun track.

The woman who, on a chance encounter, introduced me to the trail had trained for two years before embarking on her journey. So, it was disappointing to hear that she became unwell after a few days and returned home. However, she plans another opportunity shortly, hoping to fulfill her passion and complete her hike.

I shared with her that while I found the trail grueling much of the time, it felt like the journey was not about me, and the only choice was to continue. Her response was very affirming, as she noted that being willing to put myself out there and be open to the experiences was an act of passion. She said the trail is always hard and challenging, external or internal, and the joy and rewards come after. The experience and resilience that it builds stay with you forever. In addition, the journey inspires others and instills a drive to open yourself up to other new experiences.

There was a turning point where I thought I couldn't complete the hike due to fasciitis. I hobbled into Peaceful Bay after thirty-three consecutive days and traversing thirty-one kilometers of dunes, rocks, and beach, knowing that two more difficult days lay ahead. My feet had been screaming at me for days, and I knew it was time to honor their need for rest. Unfortunately, it hadn't occurred to me that I had a choice to rest before continuing; there was no accommodation and no public transport into Peaceful Bay, and it was too hot to rest up in my tent for any lengthy period. The only way out of this predicament was to get to the next town via a good Samaritan. Surprisingly, the idea of not completing the trail filled me with great sadness, given all I had been through. However, with a good night's sleep in comfortable accommodation, a foot massage, and prolonged rest, I could review my situation and realize I could continue my walk to the finish line.

Having recently read *A Walk in the Woods,* Bill Bryson's book on the Appalachian Trail, I found it remarkable how similar Bill's experiences were to mine and others I had shared time with on the trail. Bill considered that the central feature of the track was deprivation. The removal of oneself from the ordinary conveniences of life. Although he acknowledged his occasional awe at the marvel of nature, he found hiking a tiring, pointless slog between distantly placed comfort zones.

And yet he referred to hiking as a series of contradictions. Being simultaneously impressed and bewildered. Bill noted being filled with rapture and gratitude at coming into a town and accessing ordinary things such as food. I laughed aloud when he asked a waitress to give him the largest piece of pie she could without losing her job. There was a deep resonance for me in that despite the mind intellectualizing about using the towns as an opportunity to eat healthy foods such as salads and vegetables, the heavy, fatty, and sugary foods always win the day. After several days of packet soup, pasta, and muesli bars, a void wants to be filled, and salads don't do it. One delight of the walk is knowing that one can eat whatever one desires and still lose weight.

It appears that on the Appalachian Trail, one also has their share of rodent experiences, as I had on the Bibbulmun trail. Rats particularly chew for chewing; they need to keep their front teeth functional. I am sure many of us can relate to chewing for the sake of chewing. Rodents associate the shelters with people and people with food. Large supply boxes are provided to store food overnight; however, these creatures are exceptionally clever and tend to outsmart any invention that has been considered, including hooks to hang the backpacks so they dangle in mid-air.

Bill mentioned meeting a blind man who had walked the Appalachian trail with his seeing-eye dog. Despite falling over five thousand times, the man admitted that he never enjoyed the hiking part, but it was something he felt compelled to do. "It wasn't my choice," the man stated. This was remarkably resonant with my own experience of being seemingly choiceless. Sometimes the universe throws us a curveball so we don't get complacent and forget the exhilaration of triumphing over the odds.

There is this boundlessness in the woods, where every glimpse into the canopied trees and every bend in the path can seem indistinguishable from any other. I recall taking the middle of three routes on a particular section of the trail—although, at the time, I only noticed two paths and took what I considered was the one furthermost to the left. After not sighting a track marker for more than five hundred meters, I referred to the book, and the markers seemed to indicate I was on course, with a four-wheel drive track and a log landing within the distance noted. Then, after continuing and realizing it was time to turn back, I noticed the third trail, which also included a log landing and a four-wheel drive trail at similar distances. It highlighted how one could walk the same section repeatedly and be none the wiser.

Bill referred to the strange contrast of how the canopied forest became one's entire universe and how one's thoughts shifted to accommodate the here and now, with an overall focus on reaching the next shelter.

The trail is an exercise in spontaneity. One minute you encounter a downed tree, and you must find a way over, under, or around it. On one occasion during this experience, the whole back of my pants ripped away as I did an unimpressive sideways roll maneuver.

The contradictions were noteworthy. After several days, I looked forward to reaching a town to enjoy a hot shower, a comfortable bed, and cooked food. However, attending to the lengthy "to-do" list was equally exhausting, as was starting again with a heavy food-laden pack. I also viewed the trail as an endless slog that was exhausting and invigorating.

Despite the many challenges of heat, blowflies, mosquitoes, perspiration stinging in the eyes, dunes, steep and slippery terrain, trip hazards, and injuries, to name but a few, many people concur that the inconveniences often pale in comparison to the sunsets and sunrises, the abundant wildflowers with over fifteen hundred species, the birds and animals encountered, the sense of achievement after arriving at the shelter after several hours walking, the people you meet, the stories, and the passions shared via the guest book through poetry and art.

This was a poetic reflection in the guest register:

"Before this trip, he would look upon me with affection.
I could see the sparkle in his eyes that I would generate.
But while we have been walking, it has been different.
Most of the time, he has his back turned to me.
I can't seem to do anything right.
I'm to blame if he is going too slowly.
He thinks I should carry more, but I can't.
I don't know if this relationship will last.
Five years we've been together and you would think that level of
commitment would be rewarded.
But I know he has been looking at others.
I know it can't last forever, nothing does.
So, with every stitch that fails,
I feel one step closer to being replaced with a newer backpack."

Victor H

And this:

"The loving concern one human being shows to another is my most vivid memory of the walk. Sharing physical things, food, clothing, first aid gear, insect repellent, laughter, ideas, help with backpacks, and the joy in the flowers and birds. The courage of some, the growth of others, the watchfulness of most. The list is endless."

There is even a dedicated Facebook page for hikers to ask for track or equipment advice, share stories, post photos, seek support, look for lost property, or just share a laugh. For example, a recent post was about a woman seeking a home for her dog while she walks the trail. Within minutes of posting, a reply was forthcoming that fitted the lengthy criteria of suitability the woman was hoping for.

I also had opportunities to support others, such as helping those who miscalculated the number of days of food before the next town; booking accommodations for those off the grid; looking up tidal information for the inlet crossings; and offering hot water to a hiker who ran out of fuel.

I hobbled and stumbled to the finish line of Albany after incurring many injuries. The heel spurs and fasciitis were my companions and made their pain heard daily. Somehow, I lost my hat, a fly net, a pair of socks, a towel, and a pair of trousers and traded my boots for runners midway through the hike. Despite bypassing a couple of sections, I am satisfied with what I have achieved, as it allowed me to venture out of my comfort zone, lose some weight, and increase my strength and fitness.

Furthermore, preparing to write this chapter, and reviewing video posts of the trail, enabled me to gain new perspectives, and I am continuously surprised as if I am seeing the trail for the first time.

To paraphrase Arthur Miller,

"In the end, one must finally take one's life in one's own arms and surrender in a passionate embrace."

The opportunity to write about my experience has been enriching. It has deepened my appreciation for the journey, for the beauty and miracle of nature, for the many souls who contribute to the shared vision in support of something greater than themselves, and for the curiosity of a moment of ignited passion, which can lead to asking oneself, "What if it is possible!"

I'm passionate about writing this chapter with you, the reader, in mind. I hope this touches you in a way that calls you to what ignites your passion, to more fully inhabit those things that result in you living a purposeful and adventurous life.

"If you feel like there's something out there that you're supposed to be doing if you have a passion for it, then stop wishing and just do it."

~ Wanda Sykes

CHAPTER FIVE

Treasures of the Heart

By Anthony Dierickx

My first day in high school brings back many memories. I remember my mum driving me in our family's white Mitsubishi station wagon from Tanunda to Nuriootpa in the Barossa Valley. It was a familiar route, as we often drove to the local Community Shopping Centre. Lost in my thoughts, I looked out the passenger side and watched the trees and vineyards go by on this sunny day with clear blue skies. I was a ball of emotions as I tentatively waited in anticipation of arriving at the school. Finally, I was ready to go: combover haircut—check; blue school uniform—check; lunchbox and new books packed in my bag—check and double-check. I felt excited and nervous about what may lay ahead on this day.

As I was dropped off at the school entrance, I absorbed all the sights and sounds around me. Nuriootpa High School was a large school of a thousand or so students. I will always remember the reception and teacher's rooms standing on the left in grandeur, with their stone wall façades and long drawn windows like multiple eyes looking down at me. The two-story classroom building sat on the right with the ground-floor library. I later found myself reading *The Adventures of Tintin, Asterix and Obelix*, and many more literary comics. It felt like a new world, transitioning from primary to high school.

During my high school years, I was excited about the future and where it would take me. At the same time, I prudently contemplated where I would take my life after high school. At that point, I felt a real purpose and passion to pursue my dreams. I was quite inspired by my uncle, who chased his career passion of becoming a pilot. So, I chose this path and studied physics, chemistry, Indonesian, and high-level mathematics in Year 12. I also attended information nights at the Defence Force Recruiting Centre on how to become an Air Force pilot in the nearby city of Adelaide, which is about 1.5 hours away. I eventually did five years as a driver in the Army Reserves to test the daily workings of Defence Force life. I realized from this experience that I valued my freedom more. Ultimately, my dream of being an Air Force Pilot never eventuated. I then thought, what else could I do?

The same feelings of new beginnings presented when I graduated from the University of South Australia with my marketing degree in August 2014. It was a momentous occasion as I made my way onto the stage with my mortarboard cap and gown to accept my completion certificate from the Chancellor. My immediate family members were very proud of me for being the first within our small family circle to graduate from university. My grandfather even purchased a wooden picture frame for my certificate, unheard of since he was quite frugal with his money. However, since finishing my degree, I've never worked a marketing job in a full-time capacity. The only thing that came close was when I obtained my real estate license as a sales representative in 2015. I was casually helping my family's business with some aspects as a marketing manager—a job I wasn't very passionate about. So, I returned to the drawing board and wondered, what is my lifelong purpose and passion?

I won't forget the treasured moments of marrying my wife in Adelaide and Malaysia in 2016, with over two hundred attendees witnessing our special day as we hitched the knot twice in two countries. This was the scariest and happiest experience of my life. These are special memories with my wife, loved ones, family, and friends I will hold dear for the rest of my life. However, as had happened to my parents when I was ten, my marriage ended in divorce about five years later, in 2021. Again, I was left with that empty feeling, wondering, what is my true passion? That insistent question in my mind has followed me throughout my life. Follow me behind the curtain as I reveal how I turned that question from an abstract concept to a real manifestation—and continue to do so. The journey never ends!

Generally, when something is new, it feels unfamiliar and scary. I've learned from my experiences that staying frozen in fear and holding on to what is comfortable does not get us very far. Learning never stops because life is about perpetual growth as we move through our experiences. It's important to note that the climb is not about reaching a particular destination and then plateauing at that station. Fear loses its grasp on us when we accept and acknowledge it for what it is, taking action and following through with our hearts without regrets or doubts. We must learn to be comfortable with being uncomfortable. Most importantly, we must not forget to celebrate every win. This powerful strategy alone will open opportunities to live with passion that we previously thought impossible!

I remember a friend invited me to help him celebrate his birthday sometime in the early 2000s. It was special because he wanted to go out in style, wearing his full-bodied red Lycra suit while jumping from a perfectly good plane twelve thousand feet above Goolwa Airport in South Australia. At the time, I was scared out of my wits to consider jumping since I feared heights. I ended up facing my fear head-on while celebrating my mate's birthday. In hindsight, it was funny rewatching my skydiving video. The footage showed me and the experienced diver tandem diving out of the plane, and you could see the blood rushing out of my face as we dived. When we finally reached terminal velocity, I stopped screaming my head off. Instead, I was consciously present to take in all the beautiful sights below the farmland plots, surrounding hillsides, sandy beaches, and the landing strip of the country airport we had taken off from moments before. When we reached the point of diving stability, my face looked like a pit bulldog's head hanging out of a moving car window. It wasn't easy moving my head, as the force of the upward wind flattened my face when I tried taking in the views. Looking back now, I believe it was a great experience and worth breaking through my fear of heights. I look forward to pursuing more skydiving escapades as I follow my passion for traveling to other countries like New Zealand and Dubai.

> "Feel the fear and do it anyway!"
> — Susan Jeffers

During the over thirty-eight years I've been wandering the earth, I've learned that we innately have all the gifts within ourselves to achieve anything we want to accomplish in our lifespan. I believe this wholeheartedly because I've lived it. It's important to note that the leading stealers of dreams are doubt, lack of belief, or faith, resulting in us devaluing ourselves or sabotaging our success. I can talk from experience because I've dealt with constant mind games, especially when studying for my marketing degree. I would stay back late on campus, typing away on the desktop computer in the multi-level building to complete my three-thousand-word essay, buzzing from energy drinks purchased at the nearby vending machine, madly rushing to beat the midnight deadline as I pressed "submit online." During this time, thoughts arose like "Am I good enough?" "Can I do it?" "Will I pass?" "No one in my immediate family has a university degree." I had doubts you wouldn't believe me, especially since I had initially failed most of my first year of university when I was studying my first preference in IT. Believing in myself was on the lower end of the scale. It ended up taking me eight years part-time to finish my marketing degree. As the adage says, "It's not how long it takes you; it's about finishing what you started." This always reminds me of the metaphor of the race between the hare and tortoise: "Slow and steady wins the race." I share this with you because my lack of self-confidence and hyperfocus on personal shortcomings eventually led me to follow my passion for helping others break through their limiting beliefs and "imposter syndrome."

"Develop success from failures. Discouragement and failure are two of the surest stepping stones to success."
—Dale Carnegie

This is why I later learned to seriously seek the guidance of coaches, mentors, or individuals to hold me accountable for tracking my progress with my S.M.A.R.T. plus goals. They were the pillars of my success thanks to their models of best practice. By learning from the mistakes of those who had come before me, I sped up the process of obtaining my results. Modelling success is important in achieving your passions in life to avoid the whole trial-and-error experience. This is where investing in yourself comes into the equation.

I have a good friend who lives in the blue mountains of NSW. He is an astrophysicist and an anthropologist explorer of the surrounding aboriginal caves that lie hidden in the brush of the blue mountains. I've frequented there a few times, and the views from the platform overlooking the mountain ranges and three sisters— "Meehni," "Wimlah," and "Gunnedoo"—are breathtaking. I will never forget the words of wisdom my friend instilled in me: "A coach is someone who shows you the beautiful qualities you already have within yourself that you didn't know you had consciously, like shining a torch on the walls of a cave to view the indigenous paintings etched on it." The significance of the coaching sessions with my mate taught me not to let F.E.A.R. (False Evidence Appearing Real) hold me back from living life with passion.

As mentioned, one of those recent failures was my marriage, which ended over a year ago. After the initial honeymoon phase had passed with my wife, we started to see the cracks in our marriage emerge, which sadly created a toxic relationship. Unfortunately, we focused on our shortcomings rather than the good we both brought to the relationship. It was a sad affair, and without going into too much detail, we ended up divorcing in late September 2021. You may consider this to be a doom-and-gloom type of experience. However, in retrospect, I consider it to be a pinnacle moment in time where I learned a lot about myself, and dare I say, it was the largest growth spurt I have had.

From the heartbreaking end to my marriage, I went through the process of learning to "let go, let God." Considering recent events, I find this affirmation especially prevalent, with current global economic challenges happening swiftly around COVID-19, distribution issues, and inflation spikes. I recalibrated myself by learning to re-learn; rediscovering who I wanted to be and what I wanted out of life; leaving behind old identities; releasing past hurts; and ultimately forgiving myself and my wife for past transgressions. These experiences contributed to my core passion for being a life coach.

> "If we can realize that life is always happening for us, not to us…
> game over, all the pain and suffering disappears."
> —Tony Robbins

I've never defined "living my passion" as engaging in short-term hobbies like stamp collecting or completing a "walk-the-dog" trick with my yo-yo when that was the fad during my younger schooling years. I went much deeper than that by looking at my long-term drivers. I would follow these ambitions even if I had everything I could want or need. I believe we all have a purpose in life that is unique to us. When I first heard this truth from a staged event in the early 2000s, thoughts of doubt crept in, saying, "Someone has already done it," or "That's good for them, but I can't see myself doing that." Over time, I learned to be candid with myself, acknowledging the self-talk in my head while avoiding thinking about it too much so it didn't fester. That is why I have worked on focusing on myself and the 5.5 inches between my ears for the last twenty-plus years. I've found that mindset is a key component to discover your passion. This includes being in alignment with my authentic values and beliefs.

Remember that I said it's a journey; it's exactly that. The self-doubts would creep in sometimes and lead me to states of depression. This included binging on Netflix movies or TV series while eating a plethora of junk food. I don't work in half measures; if I go down with the ship, I go all the way. I was in the classic mode of self-sabotaging my success, denying myself from following my true purpose and living with passion. Close family and friends who believed in me would tell me so many times that I could succeed, but I would think, "La la la la, I can't hear you; I don't want to know." I think you get the point.

I chuckled to myself recently when I reheard the words from an old Jim Rohn seminar on YouTube: "The major key to a better future…is you," with emphasis on "major" and "you." I've looked in the mirror myriad times with a cynical smile and said, "If it's meant to be, it's up to me." When you're an adult, it is very easy to be cynical about life when you've been put through the wringer. I encourage you, though, to never give up. Instead, do some soul-searching on what your passions are. Even writing notes through mind mapping can help you collect and collate your ideas on paper. I've found it helpful to jot down a few points on my blank canvas on how to be present and take daily actions around three key areas of my life: being a life coach, professional market trader, and globetrotter.

"Mindset is an important key to unlocking your passions in life."
—Anthony Dierickx

Childlike curiosity is so powerful because it aids in manifesting new ideas either through inference or from nothing. I've gained so much by standing still, being observant, and heightening my senses, allowing me to be present in different environments. This practice has been especially relevant when I'm at my local coffee shop, watching the comings and goings of patrons. In contrast, the sounds of the coffee machine and the smell of freshly ground coffee beans permeated the morning.

One Sunday afternoon, I had an epiphany while contemplating what to write for this chapter. I was reminded of the story of *Pinocchio*, originally published by Carlo Lorenzini about 140 years earlier in Florence, Italy. I was reminiscing over the magical moment and musical phrase shared in the old Disney movie between the Blue Fairy and the wooden puppet Pinocchio: "When you wish upon a star, makes no difference who you are, anything your heart desires, will come to you...your dreams come truuueee." This statement is about believing in yourself and taking that leap of faith. I have taken that leap and continue following my lifelong dream of being a life coach on and off the virtual stage platform.

My coaching journey has taken me across the world, speaking mainly on Zoom or Microsoft Teams platforms amongst different audiences, aiding individuals or groups in unlocking the secrets of their minds in both a corporate or self-development setting. I'm passionate about the coaching space allowing me to aid others in breaking through the limitations they place on themselves.

Your why, spiritual path, internal heart compass, northern star— however you look at it—is like an itch you cannot scratch, a door beckoning you to open it. If we follow our purpose wholeheartedly, our lives will truly start, flowing in alignment with our authentic selves. Granted, there will always be roadblocks to testing and building our character. I'm reminded of a documentary I watched recently about the greatest siege battle the world had ever seen, occurring in 1453 between Roman Emperor Constantine XI and Ottoman Sultan Mehmed II. This siege battle for control of Constantinople was the turning of tides in history where the Roman Empire fell, and the Ottoman Empire rose to conquest. The Ottoman Sultan Mehmed II held out for eight weeks to siege

Constantinople after many failed attempts to overrun the Roman city via army skirmishes and cannons battering the walls. As it happens in life, the Sultan experienced failures and victories on his way to taking the city. Along the way, people doubted his actions, advising him to pack up the camp and retreat. Those dubious advisors closest to him reminded me of close family and friends who did not support me and doubted my actions when I followed my passions.

Yet the Sultan also had his entourage of staunch supporters who praised him throughout the good and bad highlights of the battle. This historical period reverberates with the truth that we should believe in ourselves regardless of what others say. I've discovered that persistence pays off when it comes to overcoming obstacles, even though, at times, it isn't easy or feels illogical. For most of us, the conquest of living our passions starts on the battlefield of our minds. Note that for over 1,700 years, twenty-three armies had failed to take the city of Constantinople (aka Istanbul) before Ottoman Sultan Mehmed II conquered it over Roman Emperor Constantine XI.

Similarly, there are pinnacle points in your life where you reach a crossroad and must either grasp the opportunity or lose it. It takes courage to follow through with your goals against all odds, including what others say about you and what you think about yourself. I say this as I've encountered roadblocks regarding the next steps in developing my website for my coaching business and the investment it will take to achieve that. Even though I don't know you, I have the utmost faith and belief that you can succeed. Focus on the WHY, and the HOW will follow.

> "Winners never quit, and quitters never win."
> —Vince Lombardi

As I grew up, I have to say I missed my creative side. During my high school years, I enjoyed investing in the arts, whether playing

Beethoven's *Für Elise* on the piano or painting silhouettes of bridges, rivers, and reeds on a blank canvas in black ink. I recently enjoyed re-exploring my artistic side by picking up an acoustic guitar and strumming it spontaneously while listening to tunes through my headphones. I find that letting go of the inhibitions we place on ourselves is quite freeing and serene. This has been especially pertinent when my best friends, perfectionism, and procrastination, visit and stop me like a stalemate in a chess game. I've learned not to wait for life's perfect moments since they never arrive. My next step is to start building my life coaching website and stop procrastinating!

Follow your passions and live them now, even if you can only take small steps forward—any small action counts towards living the life you truly want for yourself and your loved ones. And you can surprise yourself at how much small compounding steps can assist in achieving one goal after another. Your passion could be painting, music, directing short films, drawing, starting a business, changing your eating habits, riding a horse, travelling to new destinations, or whatever it may be. As they say, the world is your oyster!

As a Christian, I've learned to lean in and place my faith and trust in God. Searching through the passages of the Bible, the verse I find resonates most is, "For where your treasure is, there your heart will be also" (Matthew 6:21, NIV). Within our hearts, we can truly find our passion and place in this world. I find that it's like a magnetic arrow directing the compass towards my northern star, the vision for my life and the answer to finding my whole self. And to be honest, this may take days, months, or years, depending on your ability to be coachable and discern what is true and not true for yourself. My intimate and close relationship with our Heavenly Father and Savior Jesus Christ has aided me in defining what my passions look like for me and being content with what I see in the mirror. God has given me the vision, and I must be courageous enough to pull the trigger and follow this vision. So, watch out, world—coach, trader, nomadic life, here I come!

So, remember to believe in yourself; visualize your dreams in the present; have faith; take action daily; review your plan of action and recalibrate where needed; and, most importantly, pursue your passion no matter the obstacles in your way. I'll never forget these words of wisdom from a friend: "We can remember the lyrics of our favorite song but find it hard to recite a page from our favorite book." It's so true; music makes our life more colorful. So, go forth because your concerto, your composition of stories and adventures, awaits you to take action! Choose to be the author of your life now because this world needs the precious gifts you have to share. God bless you as you take the first step toward living your passion!

> "The last word remains with the one that never gives up!"
> —Colette Dore

"You can't find your passion in your brain. You have to feel it through your heart."

~ Marie Forleo

CHAPTER SIX

―――――∽o⌒∿⌒o∽―――――

Living with Passion—Against All Odds

By Annette Korolenko

Somewhere in the cosmos, hidden forces work on your behalf to guide you.

For as many stars that light up the midnight sky and beyond, there are infinite possibilities for you to explore your passions. Yet, somewhere within the Universe lies the mystery.

No one knows the hows and whys of your life's unfolding that will ultimately lead you to your destiny. Yet, with twists and turns on your path to navigate through, your guiding compass knows within.

So, believe there are miracles, serendipity, and coincidences waiting to happen unexpectedly on your behalf when you dream big with passion.

> *"When you want something, all the Universe conspires in helping you to achieve it."*
> *—Paulo Coelho*

Passion is an unbridled force propelling you beyond your limitations to follow your inner flame.

Nothing seems impossible, no matter what anyone says. Taking risks to answer your calling makes obstacles disappear. Regardless of age, it's never too late to have fun and live with passion, breaking out of the same mundane routine to want something more. Enter the realm of childlike wonder to find passion and spark creativity. Embark on a journey to awaken your senses and explore your imagination.

Sometimes, having less is more...

As I reflect on childhood memories of having little in material things, I realize how rich I was because less sparked my imagination and created a passion for more. This was the fertile ground for dreams to come true.

My family and I lived in a sixteen-unit apartment building in Chicago, the true melting pot of America. The tenants were hard-working, honest families of diverse cultures, making Chicago the city it is.

A coal incinerator in the basement heated the building. All the neighbors placed paper bags full of washed or used clothes outside their doors to either be burnt or given away by the landlady to the less fortunate. Times were hard for larger immigrant families, but they found ways to be happy.

I was the youngest of four siblings. Even at five, I was expected to do more than my share of chores since I was the only girl. I would pull up a chair next to the stove to cook myself eggs in the morning. I was responsible for washing the dishes by hand, helping with dinner, and mopping the floor.

My siblings and I did not receive an allowance because my parents paid for our expensive Catholic education by working at 4 a.m. each morning. So, my attending kindergarten meant wearing a plaid gray and navy jumper over a plain white blouse and walking to school a mile each way.

Watching TV was not allowed except for joining my parents on the weekend to watch old reruns of Dean Martin shows and Elvis Presley movies. I knew whom I wanted to become when I grew up: a dancer in the Elvis movie *Viva Las Vegas* like Ann Margaret nicknamed the female Elvis the pelvis. I dreamed of dancing passionately in white go-go boots and straight-leg-style pants.

On my fifth birthday, my dreams came true. The landlady discovered a treasure trove of goodies: used white go-go boots and a pair of orange capri pants alongside a gray two-wheeler bike my size. So, filled with passion, I took off like the wind on my bike, not doing chores, to proclaim my freedom.

My adventure into passion began. I undid my long braids so my hair would blow in the wind while I explored the neighborhood, riding into a sunset the same orange color as my capri pants. Zooming past houses, I could hear different ethnic music through the open windows, with some kids dancing in the streets. The scent of tacos, and Chicago hot dogs with mustard and peppers, filled the air. Occasionally, I would park the bike to look on the ground for loose change or empty pop bottles for refund coins to satisfy my cravings. Finally, I came across an interesting jagged rock, a colorful marble, and a tiny red maple leaf I put in my pockets to later hide in my shoebox under my bed.

All the kids were outside, some dancing salsa to Latino music, others attending swimming lessons, Girl Scouts, or other clubs I could not attend since I had no money.

It started to drizzle, so I took my bike into my apartment building. When I ran into the house again, I felt cooped up. Then, I heard the rain pitter-patter against the windows. I wanted to feel the energy of the rain on this hot day. So, I jumped into my pink swimsuit and ran outside barefoot, dancing in the rain. I jumped into puddles, delightfully squealing and being in the moment. This sensation of rain made me feel alive, raising my frequency to joy. Even though I was yelled at and spanked, it was still worth it to experience those passionate moments.

When Thanksgiving came around, my parents invited neighbors to a dance party to celebrate life. They had saved enough money to make a feast. The inviting aroma of dill pickles and Hungarian goulash filled the hallways, luring the neighbors to the right door. My mother had a passion for cooking and feeding everyone. She knew what it felt like to go hungry, having grown up in Poland during World War II.

The apartment walls still had murals left by former tenants from Greece. Artfully painted, there were glorious terraces surrounded by white pillars, purple grapevines hanging from the trellis, and a magnificent ocean view. It made you feel like you were on the terrace, viewing Greece. The painting inspired me and awakened my passion for visiting foreign countries.

The first guests to arrive at my parent's party were the Greeks that formerly lived in our unit. They came carrying a baklava tray, pastries filled with pecans, honey, and cinnamon. Next arrived were Italians with homemade wine, three Polish couples with flowers and vodka, and Puerto Ricans bringing rice and beans with Bacardi rum.

The last guest was a distinguished eighty-year-old gentleman, Johnny Amaya, whom we called Grandpa. He brought himself and his unforgettable savoir-faire. He was from Columbia, with shiny white hair combed back, framing his chocolate-colored skin. He always had a twinkle in his brown eyes. He wore an elegant cream-colored hat with a short brim and a black satin ribbon. His silk shirt was sage green with tropical flowers. His pants were black matte silk, pleated at the top, ready to tango. He taught me how to speak Spanish and dance the salsa and tango.

The evening began with dinner to the jazz instrumental "Take Five," an upbeat saxophone tune with piano chords and drums. All the guests were exchanging entertaining stories from their homeland.

At that moment, I had an epiphany! I knew that I wanted to be a storyteller.

The rest of the evening was filled with laughter and resembled a crazy dancing competition. The twirling and swirling of polkas, waltzes, jitterbugs, and the twist mixed with the spicy salsa and tango of Johnny Amaya.

The last dance was from the movie *Zorba the Greek*, showing the passion and fire in us.

All the men joined outstretched arms together in one line like a chain, dancing on one side of the room, and the women did the same on the other. It was a memorable performance worthy of an academy award—or at least they thought so!

As I became a young adult, the voices of older adults, parents, and teachers played back, discouraging me from becoming a dancer and writer. They echoed, "You're only 5'2; you're too short to be a dancer," or, "Writers don't make any money. You won't be able to support yourself."

In high school, I worked three jobs after school and saved every penny to travel the world. I then went to college. After I lived and worked abroad with foreign reporters as a translator, the Universe brought incredible opportunities for me to work for Inter-press, the press office in Europe, and on co-produced films. It was fun and exhilarating!

Fast forward a decade. Living back in the US, I received a grant to attend Columbia College in Chicago to study screenwriting. Unfortunately, my plans crashed just before the beginning of school. Classes were shut down as the pandemic began...

Who could have imagined that in the worst of times, the pandemic, personal hardships, and adversity could shift into an incredible journey of a personal renaissance of passion and the arts?

While completing a Master's Certification in Coaching and attending Tony Robbins Challenges, I simultaneously joined an online writing class.

One day, while scrolling on the internet, I became mesmerized by some paintings by world-renowned artist Gabriela D. Delgadillo. The colors were bright and expressive. I was drawn to the website and inspired to find out more. The rest was history, leading me down an exciting path of self-discovery through my writing.

Gabriela was also an author and invited me to sign up for an online writing class she co-led with John Spender, an international best-selling author and publisher. Writers from all over the world came together in this special circle to share their tales with different styles and flavors under the guidance of John Spender's golden nuggets of wisdom. The support and encouragement from fellow writers helped us all to spark our imaginations to go wild and take flight.

My passion for writing was never-ending. I was driven by an overwhelming desire to express every heartfelt emotion, to recapture moments in time that evoked deep feelings. In addition, I hoped to entertain through fiction and non-fiction, children's stories, and other genres, being sometimes whimsical and, at other times, serious. So, I wrote like a mad scientist on my phone, creating over thirty short stories.

Writing from the most sacred corridors of my heart encompassed expressing raw emotions of my soul, baring myself and my vulnerabilities with no filter. I shared being human by writing and dealing with this journey called life.

However, the day arrived when I had had enough!

With all my technical calamities of typing each story on the phone, things had become cosmically challenged. The software issues, viruses, no spell check, auto-writing changing my text, and loss of hundreds of words through disappearing, unsaved stories left me exasperated! Add to this the life adversities that were about to happen all at once, and I would soon be on the verge of a nervous breakdown...

*Drip, drip, drip...*the bathroom sink sounded like the ticking of a time bomb as I tried to write that night. Then there was a frantic pounding on my door at 4 a.m. Wearing a nightgown and slippers, my downstairs neighbor told me, distressed, that her ceiling had collapsed for the third time.

How could I repair it again? I had no credit cards. Preparing for my son and brother's funerals, and co-signing all their debt, had bankrupted me.

I returned to my phone and saw that my nine-hundred-word story from John Spender's writing class had disappeared. It had taken me six hours to write.

I had not slept in five months; ZzzQuil at 8 a.m. gave me three hours of catch-up sleep. I then awoke to find that my niece's face had swelled up, inflated to the size of a red balloon. I couldn't find my socks to get ready to head to the emergency room because the dog hid them. My dog, Luscious, was a hoarder and could fit under the bed to hide things.

My niece and I quickly jumped into the car. The temperature had dropped to 32°F, but I couldn't find my winter coat because it was in storage.

The car would not start; the key jammed because the starter broke earlier that month. After two hours, we got out of the car and prayed. Then, as a last attempt, I took a deep breath and turned the key. The car started. Thank you, God, for your patience.

I left the car running at the emergency room, then drove quickly to the oral surgeon for my niece's tooth extraction and infection. I had to drive fast because it was close to after-hours. Then, I heard sirens and lights flashing behind me. *Ooh noo!* It was the police. I got a ticket for speeding.

But we made it to the oral surgeon. Then the receptionist informed us she didn't accept Medicare; we would have to pay by cash. But we had none. My niece has cerebral palsy and is blind in one eye. She's an only child, and I took her in after my brother died.

The doctor heard our story. "Your niece could die from this infection," she said, adding that it looked like the child's life was hard enough. A payment plan would be accepted.

Returning home, I was told by my complex's association manager that my car would be towed if I didn't move it immediately. My twenty-four-year-old classic car had electrical and alternator issues.

I then checked my mailbox and found a guardianship court summons to remove my niece's freedom.

Please, God, I prayed, get me through this day to fight for her freedom!

We walked into the house to make smoothies. The blender made strange sounds—*eer, eer*—and then there was silence. Oh well, no smoothies. I got back into the car to pick up prescriptions from Walmart.

On the way back, the pharmacy called. They forgot one item. Another two-hour trip again.

As I walked in the door, finally home again, my phone dinged. I checked my email to read that the assessment had never arrived and was two weeks late.

I kept unraveling more...

As evening came, I sighed in relief, happy to begin my adventure of writing all through the silence of the night, or so I thought. I briefly drew a mind map to guide me into this story.

However, the software issues began soon after I started typing on my phone. *Buzz, buzz, buzz* vibrated the phone. The ticking time bomb was louder! Next, I received more buzzing messages instructing me to do four online live streams for the writing class. That feature wasn't working on my phone. The library shut down yesterday, so I couldn't use their computers. What else could go wrong? I went back to writing on my phone since my brand-new computer had fallen and the screen had cracked before I could try it out and get a warranty.

I was nearing the end of my story when my phone started up again—*buzz, buzz, buzz*. All I could think of was submitting my writing pieces for the Facebook group challenge. My passion for writing was the only thing holding me together.

My homeless friend called. She was sobbing so hard I could not understand her. "Can you pick me up? I am across the state line and don't have enough money to get on a train. I am hungry and cold. I am done! I can't take this anymore! Don't start preaching to me about God! I am going to throw myself on the train tracks!"

I felt a sword pierce me through the heart. Tears streamed down my face. I knew she was serious. She had attempted suicide twice before. The train was her place to sleep. I glanced at my phone and saved my story as a draft. My nerves were unraveling more...

After rescuing and feeding my friend, I messaged John Spender. I was distraught and said, "On my word of honor, I had written the story." He said he believed me. But, unfortunately, only part of it was posted.

I decided to rewrite all that work anyway and never give up! My passion for writing had been in my soul for decades, calling me like an echo to begin. This was my chance. Just do it, my mind commanded!

I continued to write again for a few hours. By mistake, some of my work was posted on my Facebook page for all to see. Strangers I'd just met were messaging me about my writing. An old acquaintance from Europe called me about my writing. I was embarrassed. I didn't delete it from my profile page because doing so, I had deleted my work from the group page once before.

Ding, ding, ding went my phone over and over again. When was this ticking time bomb going to explode? I was typing, and she knew I was on Facebook. So, I diffused the ticking of the time bomb. I did not answer.

This writing was the only thing keeping me from having a nervous breakdown...

After venting my frustrations by writing this piece on vulnerability and adversity, I realized how alone I was during the pandemic—typing on a malfunctioning phone, unable to use the libraries' computers. At the same time, they were indefinitely shut down and had no access to credit because they had to cover funeral costs.

I looked out the window, searching for answers. The skies had darkened, and I could hear thunder rumbling in the distance. My eyes were holding back dried-up tears, unable to flow. It felt like sand was under my eyelids.

Without a thought, I quickly grabbed my coat and started walking outside to nowhere, hoping the rain would pour so no one could see my tears in the rain. After a mile, I ended up before the closed gates of the cemetery where my son, brother, and best friend were buried. I heard the howling of a dog lying on the grave of his master. I wished I could howl too. Instead, I wrapped my hands around two vertical wrought iron bars, thinking that life on earth was a prison and the lucky ones were in a better place with no worries. The rain started pouring down, washing over me, releasing my tears to flow. I asked my brother on the other side, "Am I making the right decisions for your daughter?"

I turned to head back. I looked at the sky and saw an eagle soaring above the clouds. Was this a sign from my brother? I remembered his love for eagles. I could hear his voice telling the story, "Remember, the eagle is the only bird that will fly alone, high above the clouds, to avoid the rain. Storm clouds cannot beat the speed of an eagle. So, on some roads, you must be bold like the eagle and walk alone."

Although the rain poured harder and faster, I walked back slowly, kicking the puddles. I felt as if all my worries were being washed away. Reflecting on the memory of this story refreshed my spirit.

The falling rain in the streets, onto the roofs, and flowing through the gutters created a symphony of soothing rhythms in my soul. Then, a gust of warm wind brought with it a change. The clouds started clearing, and the morning sun was peeking through the trees. The tree branches rustled, and bright red autumn leaves landed on me, reminding me how beautiful nature is and how good it feels to be alive no matter what.

By the end of my walk to nowhere, all the darkness and clouds had been replaced with radiant sunshine lighting my path to somewhere...

Through my incredible journey within, I realized I found my internal compass to my North Star. Exploring different writing, music, and arts genres ignited my passion.

Who would have thought that my phone's malfunctioning was a blessing in disguise? Accidentally posting my stories on my Facebook profile page wasn't an accident at all within the realm of the Universe. Instead, the accidents became a magnet to attract opportunities beyond my wildest imagination.

I was honored and ecstatic to be invited by John Spender to co-author *Messages From the Heart*. The book went worldwide, shooting quickly to becoming number one in four countries: Canada, the US, Germany, and Australia. In addition, several international magazines invited me to write after reading the stories I'd mistakenly posted on Facebook.

I am now excited and curious to explore my writing adventures with a change in tone and color, reflecting a passion different from the verge of a nervous breakdown and grief.

Meraki

[pronounced mA-'rak-E] Greek (adverb)

***Do something with soul, creativity, or love; put something of
yourself into your work.***

Remember the word "Meraki." Put passion into what you do with
all your heart.

The "essence of yourself" is your magic that makes it unique.

An artist hopes to capture a moment in time that evokes great
emotion forever to relive that feeling again. With every brushstroke
dancing on the canvas, he carefully chooses colors to express his
intense emotion. The same could be said about choosing words in
writing and notes in music.

In life, just show up and present yourself and your personality
passionately how you show your essence matters, whether with a
shy smile or a smile from ear to ear. The tone of your voice, your
walk, and your openness to immerse yourself in an experience are
vital in living life passionately.

Be that passion you seek. What you seek may find you...

As the energy of your heart's desire and imagination takes flight,
remember that Miracles of the Spirit happen quickly, in God's
perfect timing. The fire has been lit and burns brightly for each of
us to launch our rocket ships into the sky to fly high.

Earthly circumstances do not limit the new paradigm of
exploration; this movement, infused with love and passion, inspires
us to reach our full potential beyond time and space,

creating a ripple effect...

Believe in your passion!

"Nothing is as important as passion. No matter what you want to do with your life, be passionate."

~ Jon Bon Jovi

CHAPTER SEVEN

∽◦◟◜◞◝◦∽

How To Use Passion –
The True Navigational Tool
Energetically Aligned to Your Soul

By Inarra Aryane Griffyn

Allow me to introduce myself so that you step into my Soul Journey.

I'm Inarra, a Visionary Spiritual Business Guide and High Priestess of Britain and Ireland. I coach high-frequency business owners to help them manifest a luxury lifestyle harmoniously with nature. I already know this is a wild title, and you need to get the measure of me and my title, which comes from living my passion.

What does it mean to live a life of passion?

To step forth into the fullest expression of your soul's desire?

How do we end up living the most mundane of lives?

It's simple: we sell out on our passion.

We choose the safest relationship, and we settle. When friends comment that they settled, you can be sure there's no passion. Like a job that we trudge into, counting the days until the weekend when we are released from boredom for a little while. This career can be well-paid and at the highest level, but the choice is money over happiness.

Many of my clients have been in corporate jobs for a long time, and the common experience among them is becoming numb. This numbness helps them cope with a dull life.

> "Passion is the fuel that inspires and drives people toward specific goals, no matter how unlikely or difficult they might be."

If there's one question I would ask anyone I'm guiding, it's "What is your passion?"

I meet clients from all walks of life, and the kind of women I find attracted to my spiritual business coaching are creators, visionaries, and artists. They met their passion very early, as did I. Their faces alter when remembering the moment that alchemically transformed them, altered so profoundly with the experience that it changes the course of their life and demands a strong relationship of texture and shadow that ordinary life does not have.

Passion is the energy that fills your sails with curiosity and opportunity.

Imagine a life of curiosity?

At nine, I wandered to the bottom of my beloved grandmother's garden in the late evening and looked up at the night sky. This was in North Yorkshire. Being up late was decadent for a young girl, and I was awestruck at the canopy of stars shining down on me. It was exciting, and I was swept up in a spiritual experience. My feelings were aroused. I was wide awake, present, and deeply connected to nature. At that moment, I knew from my soul's depths that I was aligned with the frequency of my Soul Journey. Guidance poured into me, and I felt called to my true path. The Universe downloaded into my little girl's consciousness. I experienced Goddess activation, and as I received new frequencies, my whole vision altered to what I must seek and teach.

Passion poured into my crown chakra, and I was set to follow a sacred path that began long before my birth. This was a re-

remembering of Source's response in alignment with one of its frequency holders.

So, I took the information and experience to my first spiritual teacher, Grandma Ida, and she unraveled the threads.

Out of this, she understood that something significant had happened to me and that I needed guidance and permission to follow the path not often taken. She told me of healers and witches who danced on the Yorkshire moors, naked and healing people with milk. I felt a surge of recognition. "I have to find my people." In "Dancing on the Moors," there was also a wildness, a reverence for nature, sexuality, and sensuality all wrapped up in the inspiration. This was a pull by the Universe to set my navigation system onto the stars and to experience the highest passion I could feel.

Peak experiences guide us to what we love. By their nature, rare opportunities don't often happen, which is why they stand out. Yet, if we are open to that level of our connection with our Soul Journey, we can invite them to occur throughout our lives. They are glimpses of bliss forged from human potential. The question is, "Are you living up to your potential?"

We can all have a routine, it's straightforward, but to stand on the top of the mountain connected to the stars and earth, and feel the essence of what it is to be human, planted on the planet one more time, to let that flow through, we must energetically align with what our hearts yearn for. Like a compass, these experiences map out what we are here for and what we are designed to seek.

Take note, Human: Your destiny awaits you.

From my nine-year-old self, I was set on a course for the healer's path. I had no words for it and didn't know what a healer was exactly. But in the understanding, I became a seeker of all things spiritual. By the time I was 14, another moment connected. Living in Canada by this time, as my parents had emigrated and taken me with them, I was reading magical tales of England in the books of Mary Stewart (*The Hollow Hills, The Crystal Cave, The Last Enchantment, Merlin*). I recognized the idea of the feminine fairy ally, of Merlin, and the guides who helped the king. At that time, I saw a young man in armor with no headdress looking out my bedroom window. A hallucination or past-life connection, I could look at him clearly and for some time. The next day I knew I was meant to write a book on ritual. Some experiences can't be explained, and this was one of them. The incident stood out, and I gained clarity on the fact that I was to be a writer and ritual was important. I lived the in-between, betwixt modern life and an ancient calling.

When we are in the throes of passion, the messages are spoken in emotion, not the thinking mind. But unfortunately, we don't have a language for emotion as it's a full-body expression of YES or NO in other cases!

By the time I was in my teens, I knew my top value was spirituality and that I was a seeker on that path. Anything that did not have a spiritual context felt lacking. I remember being in university, and the intellectual arguments, for the sake of intellectual proof, circular in their flow and never going to the next level of a higher purpose or vision, were empty words to me. The same rang true for politics. It didn't go far enough as a solution; it was just combative and righteous, "I'm right, you're wrong." So, I shifted my focus to passion and spirituality.

With passion as my barometer, I consciously chose to seek out the lands speaking to me. But unfortunately, my passion was not in Canada. Though I could feel many good things there, the beauty of the land, the openness, the Indigenous connection, as a location of passion, Canada was not my land.

So, at the age of 23, I traveled around Europe, starting in London, and when I finished the trip, I asked a friend if she knew of any flats to rent. She told me there was a room in her house that was a squat (a free space common in London where hippies occupied empty buildings), but it had no heating. I jumped at the opportunity. I never went back to Canada. Despite the lack of heating and only knowing one person in London, this was an act of passion. I felt the twinge of my soul steer me toward England.

You may have felt the same pull when you go somewhere and end up in a different but entirely aligned place. A character in Native American folklore, the Coyote, whose meaning, if drawn, rules the concept of Divine detour. He is considered the trickster, and you think you are going somewhere, but Coyote takes you where you need to go. In other words, you are exactly where you're meant to be. You just need to be rerouted.

For me, the passion for ancient spirituality started to open opportunities. I worked on archaeological sites in southern England and spent a year studying ancient ritual sites. I then applied for a job with a friend who told me, "It's an amazing opportunity," I didn't even ask where the job was. As it happened, I got the job and found out it was in the Outer Hebrides, Northern Scotland, for three months over the summer. Again, it was on a remote ritual site where I experienced Indigenous Scottish Ancestors from 5,000 years ago and a fertility site. In addition, we dug up a decorated stone penis. At this ceremonial site, I was taught how to experience nature as Divine and the simple concepts of ley lines and power energetics of the land.

On the Summer Solstice during the dig, I took LSD with another archaeologist, and we walked all day across the ancient land and found that every standing stone and every stone circle was positioned on the crossing of two or more ley lines. I was open to the psychedelic experience and could see other dimensions. I saw a network of energy lines where the land was more expressive. That was another day of passion. I can still evoke the memory of walking all day late into the evening with the summer Solstice sun until 11:00 pm and the feeling of exhilaration as we came upon the most exquisite stone circle overlooking the sea. It was not on the tourist trail; we discovered it through my visionary guidance system of ley lines.

"In 1921, amateur archaeologist Alfred Watkins made a discovery. He noticed that ancient sites at different points worldwide all fell into a sort of alignment. Be the sites manufactured or natural, they all fell into a pattern, usually a straight line. He coined these lines "leys," later "ley lines," and in doing so opened a world of super-natural and spiritual beliefs."
~ Katy Serena

Much later, I learned I saw the acupuncture spots of the planet. They were chosen for their energy as ritual sites, group connection, power, and expressions of happiness. Over time, monuments were built on top of them; I saw them in the raw.

Years later, molded by that experience, I still run retreats on ancient sacred sites where I ask clients to speak their intentions, meditate, and send them out to these places of power. As if by magic, this work produces incredible results with business clients. I connected it all by introducing myself to the most unlikely path by experiencing passion at these sites. It was all aligned with my destiny.

In time, I met the healers, medicine people, and witches in England. I had called them in. From my nine-year experience, I was directed to become a healer, and I followed my instinct to find those who could teach me. I became a healer magnet and met many different types of healers. At that time, I could not envision my healing journey being in spiritual business.

My life has been a series of extraordinary adventures, and I'm grateful to have experienced so many peaks. However, I sometimes must blink to remind myself that it's accurate and that the recurring truth of my life is to follow my passion. I walked the path of the healer, studying many forms, and landed specifically as a High Priestess initiated into the indigenous mysteries of Britain and Ireland. This then gave me a template of how to grow an idea or manifestation, and I used this wisdom in all areas of my life, even in business.

The healer's tools are to ride the phases of the moon, the seasons, and the teachings of the ancient festivals. For instance, you would not grow something in a winter cycle, such as a seed in January; the same is true of ideas. Rather, choose the optimum growth cycle and take time for the seed to take hold under the earth, during which there seems to be no growth. That time is about letting go, taking your hands off the process, and allowing it to take care of itself. Trust is the essential ingredient. Micromanaging and overcooking a recipe are all about lacking trust. For real healing and authentic growth, we need the Feminine pause to balance the Masculine push. The same is true in any healing process and business. "To do or not to do" is the question. Both are essential.

My clients know me as the timing queen and a visionary spiritual business coach. I work with the insights to guide them on when to launch, how to expand, how to manifest the vision, and how to connect with the right allies whose frequency of aligned energy helps move their projects into the millions and billions. This training did not come from an economics school but a mystery school. The training of a High Priestess is intense. We walk the path alone, even when in a partnership.

I learned early on to trust my instincts and feel a gut instinct for inner guidance. The same is true of the business world and my instincts around deals, joint ventures, partners, and teams. The energetics of passion have a considerable part to play as well. I do not do anything I am not in a constant state of passion about. Passion is the guidance system. When the energy drops, it's time to shift. That's the lesson. I can say hand on my heart that everything I have done for the last 33 years is in direct service to passion: spirituality, love for the planet, creativity, spiritual business, plant ceremonies, rituals of the moon, and visionary guidance to my clients.

I have altered the course of my life and business by feeling how I respond emotionally to a situation and, if it lights me up, being turned on creatively. There are ways of heightening this ability with breath work, both Shamanic and Yogic, as breath is a direct route to the emotional body. Then I say "yes" to every cell of my body. Time and time again, I listen for the full body response, and even if I'm already on what seems like a path set in stone, I am willing to change position courageously. This happened at the height of my photography career when I felt a surge of passion for doing something else. Like a divine instruction, I listened to my inner guidance and quit the job with certainty, without any idea what I would do next. Then, four days later, on the full moon, I received an email saying, "Do you want to change your life?"

That email did change my life. I contacted the coaching team who sent it, took a quiz, and they identified me as a calculated risk taker, the perfect aligned entrepreneur. I felt pure trust in this process, and they then offered me several options for study. I chose property development, having never known anything about it before. After three months, my coach gave me homework to go and buy a property.

"What? You mean to jump in and buy a property?"

The thrill of this was exhilarating and terrifying, and my coach reminded me that I had studied the system, knew the figures, and was ready to take action. My resistance soon led to the excitement of putting the study into action. Buying my first property led to setting up my property development company, and 12 years later, I had a US portfolio worth ten million dollars. Every step of the way was a stretch I never fully knew I could achieve. I started with nothing, but the passion of the ride kept me there. Curiosity led me to the next step. Gratitude kept me grounded.

This experience has been repeated so many times in my life. I have achieved many things and led an exciting life, and the theme has been that when one path fades, I don't try to revive it. Instead, I feel my way toward the next passion. In doing this, I have financially backed an eco-green lightbulb, written five books, created a yoga festival, ran over 70 international retreats, become a High Priestess teaching the ancient ways of Britain, and am a yoga teacher. After launching so many businesses working with investors and heads of banks, I chose to become a Visionary Spiritual Business Coach, teaching others to follow their passion.

Passion also led me to my Master Healer, Bobby Klein.

When the essence of curiosity piques your interest, you are aligned with passion. There is a natural affinity between curiosity and passion; one leads to another. And so, one morning in Tulum, Mexico, I woke up feeling curious. I even felt this would be a special day, though I had no plans and no reason to imagine it would be. Nevertheless, my day was my own, and I wandered to the Banana Cafe for breakfast. A couple was sitting on the table beside me, and as I took out my 35mm camera to clean it, the guy started a conversation about lenses.

The woman listened and then asked me what I was doing in Tulum. I told her I planned to run a retreat or festival there. She listened intently and then proposed to spend the whole day with me, taking me to Tulum's best spots. This was an incredible opportunity, so I thanked her. The man told me he was involved in property in Tulum and would be happy to drive us around all day. What luck, I thought, to experience an insider's view of Tulum.

The whole day was enjoyable, and at sunset, we ended our tour at a spa called Yäan Healing Sanctuary. I immediately noticed the shamanic vibe outside the spa with atmospheric water pools and the fire blazing. I then wandered into the gift shop. When I got there and saw some items for sale, I knew this was no ordinary gift shop; it was a shaman's medicine store. There were the most exquisite medicine pouches, robes of intricate embroidery, rattles, I Ching coins, magical items, and herbs.

While looking at the array of items, I overheard the woman's conversation with the lobby receptionist as she said, "Inarra must see Bobby! You must find an appointment for her." The receptionist was adamant about no spaces and replied, "He's booked for three months." She said, "Oh, there's one space available on Wednesday." My host said, "Book her in!" I'm thinking to myself, book me in for what? A massage? As I walked back into the lobby, they were both looking at me, saying how amazing it was that I got an appointment. They didn't tell me what to do. The receptionist told me it was $350, and I had a moment of "What !?" but somehow, I felt guided to trust, so I did. The receptionist looked me in the eye and said, "You won't regret it; Bobby is amazing. Hard to describe. Amazing."

That Wednesday, I was shown to the back of Yäan, outside an elegant cabin room, and when the door opened, and I experienced Bobby Klein, my solar plexus was hit with a boom! I felt his presence and thought, "I am in the presence of a master healer." So, there he was, frail-looking and mystical, as he said, "Let's have a cup of tea, and while you drink, I'll start seeing visions and speaking to you. But it's not me speaking; it's my guides."

There began our extraordinary relationship. The session was one of the most intense experiences I have ever had. He sang me into visions, speaking fluent Navajo as he spent years studying ceremonies with the tribes. I saw visions as if I was out of my body. He told me that the yoga festival I was working on would fail due to the many egos coming to me to find fame of sorts and that when I returned to England, I would experience something extremely traumatic but that I would be ok. Two horrible experiences awaited me on my return home. Bobby told me I could put this into context if I understood I was standing on the threshold, the doorway of the best part of my life. All his words came true.

After my session, we kept in touch, and he told me that I, too, was a Channeler, not of his kind, as he told me he had never met my kind before and that I was a "Finder." His guides told me what I half knew: I receive information and visions from several sources. I experience this when speaking with friends and clients and can guide them with data from past and future lives toward their highest potential. This is not always easy. I am here to heal by changing their operating systems. When leaving an old operating system behind, my clients can experience the grasping of lower energies, not wanting to transform and resist the very thing that will liberate them. It is my skill and what I see as my soul's purpose.

When I returned home, so excited by the work of the yoga festival, little did I know then how awful the experience awaited me would be. I was the target of two bullies who worked together to do a social media defamation campaign. I had been singled out as one of the organizers. The first bully was an employee of the festival and wanted to be the head of photography as he had a background in computer programming. I didn't feel he was up to the role of Head of Photography. I said no. The power of NO began a cycle of hate.

His lower energies became the lens through which his ego tried to prove himself. He had a contract with our festival that included two projects; the first was to erect tents, a minor job, and the second was to create a website for the festival. He pitched the tents and got paid for it but did not make the website, and the contract was altered. He told everyone in the yoga community that I had not honored his agreement. Joining forces with the second bully, a manager at a yoga center in London, he gathered momentum. He took me to court and lost. Hardly anyone of the hundreds of yoga teachers who had had the most wonderful experience of the festival supported me. Five people I thought were friends dumped me to keep their reputations untarnished. This experience was heartbreaking.

What I realized about the world of being in the public eye is that when you follow your passion and become a public figure, you can also expect backlash. This can be an inevitable aspect of being in the public eye, and we who stand up for our passion and get noticed will have to deal with all the emotions that come with being attacked, misrepresented, and slandered. I have heard this time and time again. Unfortunately, there seems to be a trend in communities, especially spiritual ones, that celebrating someone's achievements is a lesser interest than taking them down. It's the gossip machine in action.

So, I teach my clients to expect this somehow. I don't focus on the fear, but I get them to get used to the backlash, being trolled on the internet and attacked on social media. My suggestion is to use one opportunity to speak out because that will help you be courageous. You need to set the record straight, speak your truth, and then I recommend silence. Block and delete anyone who causes you distress. I took this lesson hard and retreated from the public eye like a wounded animal. I instead focused on plant medicine ceremonies for my healing. Bobby had said that once this was over, I would move toward my true path, that of the spiritual teacher. And so, it came to be.

Now my path is apparent. I am a healer working as a visionary spiritual business coach. Sometimes you must go to the depths of darkness to rise again with clarity and true passion. I felt the truth of Bobby's words. The festival was an initiation that enabled me to become a true spiritual teacher. I worked with him for ten more years before he died in 2022. We had plans to collaborate in a retreat, and he attended two of my retreats, but he did so much to hone my skill and confidence in channeling. I now use this in all my work. It is a deep connection that I take my body and mind through. In these states, I see solutions to world problems and guide my clients to become the best, most successful, happy beings they can be. I have achieved my passion for the weird and wonderful path I walk, and now I focus on the same for my clients.

A person's passion is my strongest desire, and I guide and help my clients to seek out and immerse themselves in their particular passion. I also use the teachings of the chakras, energy centers in the body that have far-reaching energetic uses in manifesting. The focus of someone dealing with their creativity and manifesting in the world is the second chakra in the low belly and sexual organs, the womb, called the Sacral Chakra. This chakra is associated with creativity and sexuality. The creation of life itself manifests like a light in the darkness. The womb is a space for life to spark: from nothing comes something. The symbolic imprint of the manifesting experience is that first, we need space to create, and the conditions of that spaciousness are in perfect harmony with nature. The wet juicy inner dark invites passion. Sensuality, sexuality, and creativity are intertwined in a dance. The dance of life itself and passion is the energy of the dance.

On the quest for creativity, passion is the barometer that tells you when you are in communion with freedom. We go beyond our limits for passion. It may be one of the only things we go beyond our limits besides fear. Passion, however, takes us further.

If you want to tap into passion, notice what turns you on both in the context of sexuality and what lights you up.

First, notice it, and then act on it.

Compounding passion is a technique I teach of noticing what turns you on and allowing yourself to move closer to it by saying "Yes" without knowing how. Most obstacles in your path are simply because you too often ask, "How?"

Let's drop the how and move into the energetics of yes!

To be in a flow of manifesting in your life, I ask that you identify your passions. Write them down.

For instance: sunsets, public speaking, connection with people, conversation, and travel.

I would then ask my clients to create a map of passion with these ingredients, the perfect recipe for them.

Suppose the person described above could travel to different places and create events where people connect. In that case, there's a networking gathering at sunset (let's call it the Sunset Talks) and then a public speaking gig where the events always include a talk. From there, it could become the Sunset Talks podcast, as these talks are recorded and repurposed. Finally, there's a live event and an online presence. This is how I work to take my clients into a world that runs on their passions.

When I ask people what that life would be like, they always light up and say, "It would be amazing!" That's what we want life to feel like. Amazing! Money flows when the creator of an idea is in a state of passion about life. It's not about going for the money but instead going for the happiest way you can live your life, and when it's artistically created into full expression, you can be sure the money will follow. It's not about playing small or hiding your passions.

I have been asked many times how I managed to take such extraordinary passions as the life of a healer into business. My fears of looking too weird will not shut me down. My essence is High Priestess deeply immersed in the spiritual and employing spiritual ethics, teachings, and techniques as a foundation of my life. I translate these foundational teachings into business success. Your passion is a feeling, a map of where to go, what to seek, and your legacy imprint.

Permit yourself to be weird, wild, and magnificent. Passion does not sit well with a lack of self-worth, so to dance with it, we must start from wherever we are. That's the starting point. Now. You can't get it wrong. Take what you may have seen once as rare passion and compound these moments, passion upon passion, teaching your body to trust that passion will not be a one-off but a trail of exquisite experiences. You will be creating your best life ever!

This is life when viewed with hindsight; you enjoy it to the fullest, expressing your desires throughout. It's the most powerful and fastest way to alter the world's frequency. Your routine numb life will be transformed into a life of experiencing and expecting passion to show up. And it will. It's your destiny to be a happy human.

"Be passionate and be involved in what you believe in, and do it as thoroughly and honestly and fearlessly as you can."

~ Marie Colvin's mother, on her daughter's legacy

CHAPTER EIGHT

━━━━━◦○◦○◦━━━━━

Journey to Alicaan

By Brandon Bates

L ife: Be in the moment and the feeling and know that eventually, the intensity will pass and be thought just like you.

My birthday is February 27, 1995. But I've always felt aged beyond my years. They call it an old soul. I am aware of others' definitions of maturity or growth. However, I believe in growing intentionally and that this should be the defining factor of age. One can choose to grow every second of every minute of every hour of every day, and so forth. By this definition, I have grown well into my seventies while still in this current 27-year-old container. As I write this, I am seventy-seven, to be exact. Believe it or not, I have been that age for about two to three years and counting. It's a constant battle. Remember, this is all *my* truth or actuality. I'm twenty-seven and from the Midwest. My family raised me poor, and I only realized I wasn't "living" at eighteen or nineteen. So, technically I could also say I'm only ten years old.

At the age of enlightenment, I finally thought of what I wanted and what made sense—beginning to take notice of this beautiful rhythm that developed whenever an extended hand was complimented with a welcome in all walks of nature. I played sports, which allowed me to mature my ability to assist. However, I still needed the knowledge and a passion because sports as a professional career was no longer in my vision. After further experience, I knew I was supposed to help people and travel the world. Well, the first thing that comes to mind when wanting to travel the world is how one will eat and have the means to do so. I was sure airplanes cost money, and I wasn't willing to travel by sea.

I was fifty-two at this point in my life. I realized that I was born into a company and had value within it based on its policies and how the organization operates. But, in the same breath, I knew the company didn't value *me*. Since then, I've been on a journey to find my family, eat the most amazing food like we would see on those "travel and eat" TV shows, and consume the riches life has to offer. This has formed a citrusy organic passion that burns in the depths of my heart.

As if with courageous purpose, the rarely sighted blood moon took her chance and devoured him that shines not only with fire but consistency, resilience, grace, good intent, and unconcerned opinion. I have been mistreated. However, as you grow, you find out that people only treat you the way you allow them to treat you, and as soon as you create an excuse, you'll have one.

Let's fast forward my journey by about five years. I moved to AZ on October 14, 2014, and entered a new age. Another enlightenment was through the awareness and humble nature I was compelled to accompany. Laws now governed my being. If one follows these laws, they shall be untouched until the final chapter on this plane.

While a sickness was busy altering many people's minds and situations, I could manifest my investor, chapter mentor, and business. At the same time, illness and propaganda shifted this company's economy over the one-to-two-year span. Then, in late December 2019, I was introduced to the cousin of an associate of mine.

I had been sleeping on my associate's couch since my divorce, and my son was with his mother in another state. I was painfully forced to forge ahead and continue my known path and purpose and simply know that through the power of the laws and life for the family I created would be just fine—time to face my passion. I was introduced to my associate's cousin.

The cousin turned out to be rich and made it known that he did not want to be known for his money but simply for his virtue and good nature. Noticing I was dressed for an occasion, he complimented my suit and gave me his contact. He became a mentor with much relevance since we were only two to three years apart in age, both from the Midwest, and I truly desired to be an investor on the production side of happenings. He taught me how to consider the company a system with mutual benefits. Knowing the rules or laws lets you work with the system to achieve many goals.

He asked me to feed the homeless and begin setting up a nonprofit so that he could invest and donate through the proper means. The numbers he casually tossed around as my progression intruded his vision constantly were music to my ears and have never left my brain. Finally, someone was willing to give me money for ideas I possessed. It completely opened my mind, allowing even more abundance and positive vibes to flow.

As I progressed, an idea named Covid was slipping on her apron, cutting the stove, and plating up her greatest creation yet. "Enjoy," she says, as I lost my job that I had just started two weeks before. I gained another in the department that is crucial to one living out their passion and surviving anywhere they might journey: Agriculture & agri-landscape and the teaching of these subjects as well.

There was some time in between jobs. All the while, I didn't see a disaster happening. Instead, I saw an opportunity to build over a piece of the economy that was burning and producing ashes at an alarming rate. The ashes of the thousands of jobs are being lost daily and homes monthly. It was time for me to take the opportunity communities to bear and build with it.

I woke up one sunrise and went with my impulsive but somewhat intuitive sense to set the intention to attract a like-minded ally with an idea or invention. Next, I confirmed with my investor. Making sure that if I had a good idea, he would support me fully. Immediately after, I sought to find someone who had an idea or an invention, and a few weeks later, I met a woman with an invention. She was a hair stylist, an entrepreneur, and a farmer.

After a few weeks of productive banter, she introduced me to Spaces of Opportunity, or SOO, a local farm created by and for the community in the heart of South Phoenix. Please feel free to visit; just google the address. Here I found the Tiger Mountain Foundation or TMF. This non-profit organization was founded to allow folks to live out their passion, and I loved it! There were so many people who looked, including the founder and many of the farmers I had met. But one might ask, how do you know you are on the "right path" throughout life, or even daily? I truly felt aligned with the present despite everything I may have ever felt in the past regarding doubt and any lack of purpose or path.

TMF is an enzyme to my success and has been to so many over the years. In the beginning, it was given to me in what we called "loving spoonfuls," and I quickly worked my way up to the head of the organization along with two others, still inexperienced when it comes to business on a professional level but plenty of polish on a basic social level. So, I decided to be as quiet and reserved as possible to remain clandestine for a little longer. Each time we worked, I would give a small piece of my True energy with a joke or exotic laugh to one of their jokes. Then, however, I would return quickly to intentional silence. At this point in my journey, I have a natural passion, and I know you can learn twice as much from listening as you can from talking.

We documented and filmed our sessions for a docu-series with TMF and talked about critical topics that relate to everyone as we navigate this life. We worked in multiple gardens, farms, and even backyards. Yet, I've always known that the answers are in nature's simplicities and intuitive manifests.

With these actions creating decent income as time is spent, I was able to apply a "Plan-Do-Review" model making room for true progress on this Journey to Riches. Now, learning how to build something the people will visit. When you create something for the people, you must genuinely have the hyper-local community in mind that will utilize that something. If you're being honest and progressive, that eventually means everyone, which means you must accept everyone to learn about them and how something will or won't relate to them. Is what you're creating helpful to the community it resides in?

The second thing I learned was that budgeting was the number one problem for most of our people, including myself. Though I viewed myself as a senior investor since I had been doing it for about six years straight with minimal results, I felt equivalent to a middle-class man who had invested in stocks over the past decade and still went to work every day and lived paycheck to paycheck. Along with budgeting came the concept of building a sustainability portfolio and using different methods like stocks, homes, and other piles of equity to create large estates. For someone who has never heard these terms this way, imagine four jobs, each paying you the same full-time check for only a fourth of the time worked. Allowing your current income to quadruple.

Third, I learned how to shape my efforts better to be the change I want to see in the world. We must acknowledge this man who sought to make a change and see a better world for his people and all people and achieved success in many ways. I can't speak for him but I can speak to his work firsthand. I am gifted in the art of communication and negotiation. Darren Chapman roams the earth with purpose and jewels to give to those who come in peace.

To learn that in our history, individuals like Malcolm X and Martin King JR were targeted and or even hated for the message they spewed. I always thought that to change the world; I would die for it and be a martyr for my people, which I didn't fear.

Darren has helped me realize that I can enjoy life and make a change also. I grasped the true concept of moderation.

Finally, as a young boy, my mother once had us work in the garden in the backyard of the house we grew up in. I don't remember much, but I do remember dirt and shovels. I'm assuming we were pulling weeds, and miraculously we flash forward to big red tomatoes in the kitchen sink months later.

When I started to learn how to grow food, it was humbling, and it is a skill we should all know. However, I loved my hands soaking in the soil while the bugs ran all over.

¡Con Cuidado! Watch out for the ant piles because they can ruin your experience if you don't. This ant hill was not too far from our plots, and I was asked to work on the tractor near the hill for a neighbor. It was my first time using a BCS tractor, and I stepped into an ant home without proper calf-high boots. I destroyed it, unfortunately. Then added about seventeen ants to the left side of my wardrobe. Before I knew it, I was reenacting Richard Pryor in '79, trying to get the "change out his pocket."

My job was to teach everyone who visited about the history of TMF. They must support our actions: combating food deserts and nurturing underprivileged, beautiful human beings. I also taught them how they could actively support and encourage support by donating their free time to work with us in the gardens, as well as their money, and spreading the word.

The land we were standing on was a true inspiration for me. Farming was something I enjoyed, loved, and adored. It is my passion. Everyone that has seen me in that setting would vouch for that.

J2R -

I love the idea of turning your earnestness into stability—more even; generational wealth, education material, and feasible for all to benefit from. My life has grown through my purpose, and I have had to grow and truly change my thinking about passions and sustainability...

Helping people is not something you receive a reward or praise for. Especially when it really counts, or it wasn't even necessarily there to be given initially, but it still was. Staying aligned with your purpose keeps you away from harm and negativity. This is important when you are figuring out how to create a foundation. For example, understanding that next, everyone consumes real estate, transportation, and food will lead you to create a stable frame built on laws and principles that can be verified.

A quick story to convey my message. While working for TMF, I met one of the most beautiful people, a man named Harold Lloyd Gossett. He was seventy-eight, very intertwined with the organization's fabric, and would fire you right before your shift if he didn't like your attitude that day. When we first met, I gazed upon his brown, aged, yet still-smooth face. He also had some incredible eyes that helped light up a room when he smiled. However, he was old; when you start to look old, your face tends to frown regularly until you smile. I know what you're thinking, and relax. I view old as how you look, not your age, hence the frowning. You can be older than all and still be young, right? Take care of your mind, body, and spirit; you will be young forever. To continue, we proceeded with a normal greeting as if I wasn't being groomed to be one of the faces of the organization.

By the time that information was pieced together in his mind, I had already started to learn about the different personalities I would be building alongside. There were other amazing characters with whom I now had the pleasure of feeling their energies and hearing their thoughts, from the Darrens to the Brandon James, to the Macks, to the babies that would come with their parents to learn. As time passed and our relationship remained rocky, I can say I took Harold for granted and viewed him as a case to eventually nurture instead of giving him his flowers and ultimately leadership over what I planned to do as the new head farmer.

Did I mention I had no experience in farming? Though I thought I'd had some in the community, which is why I was chosen. Through the leadership in the community and building through rough patches with someone like Harold and many others, I could see how much I had to learn when it came to communicating effectively and growing anything efficiently. Harold and I didn't get along because I didn't assess the situation correctly. He is an elder, giving him much knowledge and awareness about growing food and life from a personal standpoint. I showed my lack of awareness and communication abilities without consulting him before asking to do work. He also cussed me out a few times off the clock at the watering hole. As I learned my faults, we became best friends and remained close. I would pick him up early in the mornings and ask random questions to learn about the times and what it was like for him growing up. We began to grow in our respective ways. I, as a leader and business operator, and he, as a leader and a person.

Love you, Harold!

As the real estate was becoming more and more feasible for my bandwidth to tackle, I read books and asked questions while keeping my thoughts and social gestures to myself. One day I asked Harold what he knew about the housing market. What was it like when he was younger? He first mumbled that he bought a house for seven thousand right in the heart of South Phoenix. This was in the sixties and the Phoenix, AZ area, and to this day, the market stands over three-hundred thousand for just the average price of a home. That said, you can count on your foundation being your property and producing high yields for many years. Then you can appropriately proceed with further lucrative investments and passions.

As I searched for many jobs for people pursuing their passions, I realized most of the workforce was just a step above the "lower class." Let me explain; most folks were a check, an undone dish, a late payment, or simply a wrong maneuver away from being homeless or without reliable transportation. Which then leaves them in the realm of without and scarcity.

In the same breath, I learned there were always two-three—we'll just say five out of about every hundred or so folks—that exhibited true signs of consciousness and just needed small, specific additions to center their beings from multiple perspectives; social, spiritual, financial, and so on. This confirmed that many do not live their lives through their passion, purpose, or remotely to their fullest potential. There is no foundation; if there is, it is fragile and may collapse. I was determined to find my passion and build my legacy. It truly grew into a desire.

Final thought:

I have faced calamity, racism, love, and self. Many people continue to tell me I'm not thinking clearly or have my priorities mixed. My little brother passing in 2019 was certainly an example of mixed signals, confusing Q&A's, and overall chaos when I think back on how I felt and decided to deal with the loss.

Whether the "many people" are right or wrong, I learned it doesn't matter because it's not their life to live or judge. Although everybody begins reevaluating their life once they lose a loved one, I don't think we will ever cherish death like birth. But I think they both will continue to overwhelm us sometimes. I know they will force us to think more than once.

Be in the moment and the feeling, and know that eventually, the intensity will pass and be thought just like you.

Live your passion!

"Love what you do and do what you love. Passion is the key that opens the door to joy and abundance."

~ David Cuschieri

CHAPTER NINE

Invest in Yourself

By Patrick Richard Garcia

T he thought of ending my life rose like a nightmare on June 15th, 2019 – just two days after my favorite sports team, the Toronto Raptors, won their first championship in franchise history.

I recall missing that special moment when I was sleeping off my decision to mutually end the traumatic heartbreak I was enduring with my former partner for nearly seven years. I felt bombarded, as if every emotion appeared in all corners and crevices of my life. I didn't know what to do. Interestingly, this situation wasn't my first encounter with suicidal thoughts. But every attempt to commit suicide intensifies with the transitions and key stages of life when there isn't a stable routine in place. I realized I was not living with passion for my own life but for someone else's.

It was more painful to experience not fulfilling what I desired for a long time. This circumstance needs to be the game changer. I considered all my options while navigating what I was passionate about. It was challenging. I couldn't pinpoint what drives me day to day. I always put myself last and others first. My initial impression was that all areas of my life were in ruins, especially my physical and mental health. I needed to take care of that before I could see what I could recuperate regarding time, commitments, and damaged relationships during my previous relationship.

I had a treasure chest filled with dreams in the graveyard of my ambitions that I had kept hidden for so long. These were dreams that I would never think of pursuing. So, I hired a fitness coach and a nutrition coach to build up a routine again so that I could determine the direction of my life. I needed to do this, I thought, to move forward in identifying my purpose and mission with passion.

Re-discovering my passion and purpose required me to revisit my learning disability journey. It fueled me to reflect on my commitment to chasing continued success, which I used to help others on a similar path. I didn't know what success meant for me or what to do to achieve it, but I knew I had to transform my body physically and mentally to clear out the damage I had done to myself. To tap deeper levels of inspiration and passion, I relied on the perseverance muscle I had built for 23 years, starting at age five.

Perseverance was my superpower, and I needed to tap into that. With this as my asset, giving up was never an option! Tagging along with my perseverance was my determination to see the vision come to life. I wanted to see my progress in losing weight and having more mental clarity and passion for accomplishing my dreams. The learning process was something I needed to incorporate daily and pursue at my own pace. I was eager to learn and wanted to do so quickly. But I knew that rapid progress was not feasible, as it had been long since I'd done any self-care like this.

My learning curve has always been different at different stages of my life. As a result, I tend to grasp concepts and new skills much more quickly. Being very adaptive in new environments is one of my key strengths. Using this opportunity to understand what I needed to learn besides the lessons of heartbreak and searching for answers, I came across the idea of mentorship again. I had some mentors during my university years, but they did not help me move the needle in achieving what I needed to do in life. Don't get me wrong – I had three, which pushed my self-confidence and passion for living to the next level. (The other ones, not so much. I felt they were there to build the experience on their portfolio and mark time.)

I discovered I could re-create a mentoring method that works for both parties! I didn't know I could repurpose it my way, as I follow general guidelines that suit the students and can still generate overall impact. In the following narrative, I will give the sequence of reigniting my passion, focusing on five components: Recalling my First Two Mentors, Restoring Mentorship in my Life, Trusting the Process and Letting Go, Trials and Tribulations with Full Acceptance of the Journey, and Lessons Learned.

First Two Mentors in my Life

During my university years, different people guided me and shared their experiences navigating my years as a student. I didn't have any specific mentors that would give me paradigm shifts and perspectives I never expected myself to have. I knew there had to be more to life than just the cliché: go to school, get a job, get married, build up your retirement funds, have children, retire, and then hopefully live for a while until you die with no severe health complications. I wanted to live with passion on my terms. I encountered three critical figures early on in my mid-20s who transformed how I viewed life: T Harv Eker, JR, and Loren Ridinger.

T Harv Eker was the individual that changed my views on money, even convincing me that being a millionaire at a young age was achievable! I encountered him while searching online, exploring my passion for making money. I bought his course on Secrets of the Wealthy, and it was so informative that I questioned everything I'd been taught about money! It seemed hard to believe. However, upon reviewing my financial history, I accepted his teachings, though not enough to manifest them daily.

JR and Loren Ridinger were a passionate power couple that ran a networking marketing company called Market America – SHOP. COM. I was familiar with the network marketing scene when I first learned of them. I had already been approached by many friends with similar opportunities and understood their systems. I reviewed their payment structures, attended team meetings, tested their products, and felt the long-term compatibility. However, only

Market America was a seller since one of my old grade-school friends contacted me about it, and I saw their company blueprints.

Fast forward to my acceptance as a distributor partner in July 2013, purchasing the fast-growth package. I also prepared to attend their first big event in Greensboro, North Carolina, the following year – their annual convention in the Greensboro Coliseum. I finally met the Ridingers at this convention, a major highlight.

It was surreal to see them both on stage, together and separately. I felt their power individually and as a couple was refreshing and welcoming. They were the ones that I looked up to when it came to building something special with someone – my partner at the time.

I saw their passion for one another and their commitment to the company and their family. JR Ridinger was a force to be reckoned with. His entrepreneurial spirit was extraordinary, his wealth of knowledge was incredible, and the drive to succeed was present in everything he did! I took plenty of notes whenever he talked and tried applying one or two concepts in my life. His wife Loren was similar. She was a powerful influencer in her world, building her portfolio of connections with celebrities and partnering with their products and brands.

As I intertwined the knowledge of business/entrepreneur and financial wealth fundamentals, it was evident that not everyone would understand the information I shared. I was sometimes called crazy or delusional – words I am not used to hearing. Learning from these three individuals made me realize that the mindset differs greatly between the middle class versus the rich. This knowledge ignited a passion within me to transform my generational path to a better situation in the future. However, that was kept underneath the surface, eventually buried in my dream graveyard.

The Importance of Mentorship

Without the role of mentorship in my life, I wouldn't be here presently to write about it in a book. The input from my mentors gave me hope that I could accomplish anything when I put my mind to it! Unfortunately, my last mentorship encounter was in December 2016, after which I returned to mediocrity. Without mentorship guidance, I worked endless hours in a college program that didn't align with my calling. It was not until three years later that I encountered another mentor to help me pull my life together – a mentor named Grant Cardone.

He was someone with whom I could relate, who had the vision that I couldn't see myself. I remember searching for a mentor on Google, and his name popped up. His marketing program with Frank Kern and his learning courses were offered as part of a free test trial. I bought it, and the rest was history. It was ironic because, looking back, I already had my first mentors mentioned earlier. The difference was that I wasn't in a group coaching session led by him (Grant) and his executive team boosting everyone's passion for living their best life.

Being part of his mentor program from then on forever changed my life. After so much time lacking direction, the right connections, no intent/purpose, and spending money unwisely, it felt right. It felt right to be around Grant Cardone, his executive team, and his wife, Elena—another power couple in my repertoire. The caveat of mentorship is that too many mentors to learn from, build on, and emulate will be confusing and lead to information overload. Also, our brain can withhold so much information that we tend to get analysis paralysis in figuring out how to apply what we learned. So, I limited myself to five mentors – one for each area I need to improve drastically and passionately focus on.

Being around my mentors and meeting half of them in person, I fully understood the real impact of being a mentor. They are champions, from the books they create to their expertise in the industry. I see the real value of becoming one myself. Currently, I am not at their level to similarly share the same information; I don't yet have the expertise or relevant life experience. However, I am a champion in the industry of learning disabilities and speech impairment. Initially, I did not acknowledge my years of experience. I labored under the shadow of imposter syndrome, which has lingered throughout my life, and I felt inadequate to share it with the world.

However, not stepping into your mission and purpose harms yourself, your passion for life, and your loved ones because being afraid to impact people's lives becomes daunting instead of positive. Therefore, I would recommend that everyone can be a mentor once they feel sufficiently confident if they believe in their calling and the problems they solve in the world. That's when mentorship becomes an essential aspect of life.

Finding a mentor can be a transformative experience for anyone looking to live with passion. Taking action and actively seeking potential mentors is important to begin the process. This can involve researching individuals in your field or industry, attending networking events, or contacting colleagues or acquaintances who can offer guidance. I found my mentors through books I read and conferences they ran or participated in. I worked to be part of their mentorship programs and attend events that included them as guest speakers. Although this route was more of a heavier financial investment, my goal was to work with them and take whatever steps were necessary to get there.

Once you've identified potential mentors, it's important to take steps to build a relationship with them. This may involve setting up regular meetings to discuss your goals and progress, asking for feedback on your work, or simply showing a genuine interest in their experiences and insights. Finding a mentor is about being proactive, open-minded, and willing to cultivate a meaningful relationship to help you achieve your goals with energy and passion.

Fall in Love with the Process and Spark your Passion

Much of this commitment is the self-improvement work involved in changing the environment we're accustomed to. This includes the people we spend time with friends, family, relatives, acquaintances, co-workers, and, importantly, anyone that is not contributing to our life. I needed to do all that to peacefully appreciate my boundaries and remove negative people that aren't in my best interest and mental health. My mental health has been heavily burdened for so long that I couldn't feel much pain or stress at times of difficulty because of how accustomed I am to it. That required formulating better habits and eliminating limiting beliefs to integrate new ones and live with passion.

The amount of hidden growth in doing all that work is beneficial and rewarding, but it all comes with a price. The price is sacrificing the present for the bigger deal of the future. Growth takes courage and consistency to grasp the results in smaller amounts leading to incomparable main development. Additionally, not being frequently challenged produces a higher chance of complacency and obscurity – being unknown. It's absurd to remain obscure; it tells us you want to be like everyone else, following orders from someone else and staying where you are when the world is constantly changing. That, to me, is 100% denial and lack of acceptance. We were designed to do greater things on this planet than that.

Yet, the programming from the beginning of our existence to the current state I was in – history repeats itself. I mentioned obscurity because I was in that position for much of my life, and I didn't comprehend the harm being done. But assigning blame will not make the situation any better. All I can do is complete my life's required steps and move forward. I'm developing the right schemes to obtain a prospering environment by converting my perspective to a more forward-thinking and positive mindset. Passion comes from all components of living and suffering. By drawing everything from it – the lessons, pain, and mistakes – I can compile a blueprint that will be used to execute the life I've longed for.

Following one's passion has become increasingly popular in recent years. It is a powerful concept that encourages individuals to pursue their dreams and do what they love. We are more likely to find fulfillment and happiness when we follow our passions. However, it can be challenging to figure out what our passions are and how to pursue them. It requires self-reflection, exploration, and a willingness to take risks. One of the benefits of following one's passion is that it can lead to a sense of purpose and meaning in life. Doing something we love makes us more likely to feel engaged and motivated. We may also find that our work positively impacts others, which can be incredibly rewarding.

Another advantage of following one's passion is that it can lead to personal growth and development. When we pursue something we care about deeply, we are more likely to be open to learning and trying new things. We may also develop skills and knowledge to apply to other areas. Of course, following one's passion is not always easy. It may require sacrifices, hard work, and persistence. There may be setbacks and challenges along the way. However, the rewards of pursuing one's passions can be significant. They can lead to a more fulfilling and meaningful life, where we do work that we truly enjoy and positively impact the world.

Trials and Tribulations with Full Acceptance of the Journey

Passion requires everything and all of it! That includes completing the shadow work, self-development, whatever term you want to use – to amplify the overall effect of that passion. It will establish results obtained based on the inner product, embracing the resolution of the past. Most of us understand that without planning to improve ourselves regularly and as needed, we will end up trapped in the shell of our former selves. I can't imagine we want to go through that again.

One example of undergoing tremendous challenges and tribulations all within one year was my experience as the Founder and President of a student group called Poetic Exchange, a spoken word/poetry group. Many occurred, including relationship problems, family tensions, last-minute final semester decisions, and even a big conflict with my executive team. This did not support my move to bring our school to compete in a North American spoken word competition/invitational for the first time in history.

I was in it for the long game and knew everyone needed to be there, including myself. To bring people and have them experience something once in their life or even beyond drove me to keep going despite the opposition. It felt so powerful completing and going through it all. I was prepared myself, as a competitor and an individual, as I put myself last over others. The pile-up of emotions and preparation for my contributions to the spoken word team was overwhelming. Finally, I was selected as the X-Factor poet in the semifinals – then the pressure was on!

I reworked my poetry piece, led by my poetry coaches, and practiced every five to six minutes! I was reviewing, reciting every word for word, mastering the art of pronouncing and adding character and themes to it. It got to the point where I repeated it almost in my sleep. But when I was called up to the stage to perform my piece, I blanked out and stumbled. I was devastated—intense emotions were running through my mind, embarrassingly rehearsing my piece and struggling to compose myself. Ultimately, I walked out on stage and broke down in tears. My team comforted me, but I failed. I worked extremely hard, and I flunked terribly. But, overall, the experience was unforgettable, and the passion from that moment – difficult though it was to endure – has radiated through my life to this moment.

It was a long journey, from bringing up the idea to figuring out how to create a competitive team in a short timeline, aggressively finding the funding, and convincing donors that it is all for promoting Ryerson University (currently Toronto Metropolitan University). While dealing with my handful of challenges, I ensured the idea did not succumb to inactivity because of my problems. On the contrary, I was the driving force behind everything and embraced the process! I will never forget that one day I wanted to give up the idea and forget all the hard work dedicated to it. However, the result was in front of me. It was bigger than me and was for the future of Poetic Exchange and other people who had fought to experience this event, which could change their lives forever. How crazy was that!? Was I fighting for something bigger than myself? That is how we ignite the passion within us.

Part 2: The Lessons Learned

I experienced some key failures and trials – in particular, four separate categories: failed relationships, solitude as profound strength, questioning my decisions, and the full scope of improvement in all areas of life.

Relationships: The value of relationships, including those that have not succeeded, is immeasurable. Even failed relationships can teach us vital lessons about ourselves and others. It's important to remember that not all relationships are meant to last forever, but each contributes to our growth and understanding of the world. Cherish the good memories and learn from the bad ones, for they all shape who we are. Relationships are a fundamental aspect of the human experience, and even when they don't work out, they can still hold immense value.

Healthy relationships are part of the human experience. Like every human, I have always wanted to feel included and appreciated. I was passionate about sustaining fulfilled relationships with everyone I consider essential to me! Unfortunately, great relationships also come with failed ones. My failed relationships involved not consulting my trauma inventory and choosing partners to please others, e.g., family. I adored the women I was with no matter the duration; each relationship was an experience I would never forget. They taught me how to be a better man, partner, listener, and more – experiences that would serve me well in future relationships. I was still new to the romantic relationships scene and relied on people's experiences and dating apps for advice, not other experts in this field. However, my earlier relationships romantically, professionally, personally, and spiritually failed because I did not apply the same passion, dedication, and commitment to them. Every relationship builds upon one another and has the same aspects of continuing to grow.

Solitude as Profound Strength: Embrace the power of solitude. These words may seem daunting to some, but for those who understand the importance of being alone with your thoughts, they hold a special meaning. Solitude is not just about being physically alone; it's about finding a space within yourself to be free from distraction and truly connect with your inner self. It's a time to reflect, meditate, create, and dream. In our fast-paced world, it's easy to forget the value of solitude, but it's essential for our mental and emotional well-being.

Channeling the inner energy of solitude became a life-changing aspect during the pandemic shutdown from the beginning of 2020 to the end of 2021. Finally, I understood the importance of being in isolation, a strength I wish I had known about earlier. It helped exemplify and expand the dreams I was passionate about for so many years that lay dormant!

Having solitude in my back pocket became so influential because I will not be swayed by society and other people telling me otherwise! I began to understand why I needed to protect that energy with heart and integrity to awaken my passion for life. Others often try to decide for me if I do not have the right mindset and intentionality. When others dictate my direction, my passion dwindles until I regain composure. With the reliance on self instead of others, I was more compelled to undergo more self-work, laser-focused on my goals, and appreciate every moment I must find opportunities to indulge in any form of personal growth! It was my mantra!! Solitude was my anti-depressant, a real form of happiness and character-building.

Questioning Decisions: Self-inquiry and self-doubt are two concepts that are often confused but quite different. Self-inquiry examines one's thoughts, feelings, and beliefs to better understand oneself. It is a practice of constructive self-reflection that can lead to personal growth and transformation. On the other hand, self-doubt is a feeling of uncertainty or lack of confidence in oneself. A negative self-perception can prevent us from achieving our goals and fulfilling our potential. So, while self-inquiry can help us overcome self-doubt, they are different.

It is important to cultivate self-awareness and mindfulness to differentiate between self-inquiry and self-doubt. By paying attention to our thoughts and emotions, we can recognize when we are engaging in self-inquiry and experiencing self-doubt. With practice, we can shift our focus from self-doubt to self-inquiry and begin to see ourselves in a more positive light. In short, self-inquiry and self-doubt are two distinct concepts that require different approaches. By practicing self-awareness and mindfulness, we can learn to differentiate between the two and use self-inquiry as a personal growth and transformation tool.

Decision-making is calculated and assessed; usually, questioning them is not a factor. However, there were always moments when my decisions were compromised, and I was insufficiently firm. It was evident from the lack of experience and situations that were not diversified enough to provide me with the level of confidence required. If I put passion into anything I do, there shouldn't be any second-guessing. Therefore, I thought it would be natural to decide without composing any game plan.

I was not firm and confident enough to stand by my decisions. I needed to learn how to be more affirmative. One example was inquiring about mentorship from someone in the public space and becoming myself in the long run. The decision was non-existent because I was so confident, and the solution was in front of me! I cannot pass this opportunity, EVER! Passing over too many options because of insufficient information or commitment isn't enough. Making decisions comes down to recalling my mission and passion for committing to a better life. It set the tone and foundation to allow my passions to thrive and prosper!

Full Scope of Improvement – All Areas of Life

Everything in life affects everything else. Every choice we make and every step we take has a ripple effect that extends far beyond our immediate surroundings. Whether we realize it or not, our actions can impact us, those around us, and the world. It's a reminder that we are all interconnected and that every action can create a chain reaction of positive or negative consequences. Consequently, it's important to be mindful of our choices and their potential impact and strive to make choices that will create a better world for ourselves and those around us.

To be the best version of ourselves and to give the best lifestyle to those we love and care for. That is where passion lies: it drives us to improve in all areas of life. I remember when I was working a lot to make money, spending time with others only when I could schedule it. I compromised everything from physical and mental health to recreational, family, and spiritual. All of them were drastically hit, which affected my progress; I was running in the "hamster wheel" without a direction. My passion started to die off, and my life deteriorated. When I encountered Grant Cardone as my new leading mentor and read his book called *The 10X Rule*, it gave me an eye-opening shift in the perspective that having all areas of your life filled is healthy. I had been taught the opposite – that sacrificing one or two areas of your life to get the rest was a balancing act and 100% unsustainable.

To keep my passion and balance intact, I needed to commit to attaining all areas of my life and continuously prioritize them. If no one else can lead by example within my family and circle of friends, I will be the first to do so! Passion is not only an emotional state of mind. It reminds you what will drive you through any obstacles or challenges. If everyone depended on passion for carrying them through, everyone would live an easier life. So, invest in yourself, embrace the power that your passion gives you, and follow through with massive action!!

"If you can't figure out your purpose, figure out your passion. For your passion will lead you to your purpose."

~ Bishop T.D Jakes

CHAPTER TEN

Where's Your Passion?

By Anne Henning

Yikes, a chapter about passion? How do I even begin? This used to be my least favorite question ever asked of me. I even half-heartedly considered ceasing socializing so I wouldn't have to answer the repetitive question, "What do you like to do for fun?" My first reaction was to pass on even writing this chapter because I had yet to define my passion. However, something inside me convinced me to say yes to this opportunity. This was perhaps my chance to discover my passion and let others know they are not alone if they find this "passion" topic daunting. Being uncomfortable is a sign of expanding self-growth. My chapter shares my message about choosing your reality. Perhaps you, too, will be inspired to define your passion differently. In the meantime, it's okay *not* to have a passion. You might not see it yet.

The mission of finding my passion is a beautiful dance, and the music keeps playing. When one becomes spiritual, enlightened, or has enough peace to ponder life beyond their day-to-day lives of the mundane, the topic of passion arises. This is what happened to me. I no longer said this was how it was, and I realized I needed to create my reality. I had a choice. So, what did I want to choose? What motivates me? What inspires me? What is my *passion*?

"Find your vibe, find your tribe" is a phrase I love. Until you find like-minded individuals, life can be a lonely, confusing, and even scary journey, especially when breaking away from the collective views you may no longer share. "Live your passion," my tribe championed. I started receiving this message over and over. Guides, oracles, and even my social media feed preached this message. What about when you don't know your passion? Do you lack passion? Does it have to be found? Is it always in you? These are the questions I had. After soul searching, procrastination, and reflecting, I believe passion is always in you. You must allow yourself the green light to acknowledge it. Passions are also forever evolving, some faint, some strong, and some so interwoven into your daily being that it's sometimes hard to pinpoint them.

I remember when the iPhone first came out. You should have seen my passion. First, I demonstrated to others how the phone could tell you the weather, take a picture, and about its cool map feature. Then with a beaming smile, I would show people the phone. Some would even ask me if I worked for Apple. My excitement is infectious. The next time I encountered them, they had an iPhone themselves. So perhaps excitement indicates passion?

My other passions include garage sales and cleaning because I was excited about doing them. But with that logic, do I dare call mint chocolate chip ice cream a passion? We judge our passions. I thought I lacked passion because the things that lit me up were not of the exotic sort, like horseback riding and artistry. Now, I realize passions are the things I light up about when sharing! I wonder when speaking about spirituality, mindset, intention, and the 5D. This clicked when conversing about these topics, and my friend suddenly said, "I have no idea what you are talking about, but I like listening because I feel your excitement." Passions fluctuate, but my passion is as simple as "just being." I believe the joy and happiness of one person affects many others around them on a vibrational level. So, it is a blessing to others for you to be at peace.

What do I mean by "just being?" I mean waking up with a smile, enjoying my freedom and flexibility. I have accumulated many exciting experiences through travel, but my most cherished memories are when I was sitting on my parents' back porch in

Illinois. The invigoration of all my senses makes this memory special—a beautiful breeze on a fall day. Drinking bubbly homemade kombucha is better than any unique limited-edition flavor from the store. I saw a green that I sporadically forgot existed after living in the Las Vegas desert for 19 years. Watching the wind blow through the leaves, appreciating the negative ions, and smiling when glancing down to see a variety of dogs by my feet simply doing the same thing.

I felt grateful for being able to sit in this stillness with conscious awareness and embrace the present moment. For a moment, I was not anxious about the future or remaining stagnant in the past. Waking up calm and peaceful, ready to live the day without judgment of myself. This is what I want to share with others. Allow the simplest thing to be your passion. Choose not to question yourself if you lack the fury of passion that makes you want to jump out of bed. Don't blame yourself if you even have too much passion. Clear all the validations, comparisons, and expectations regarding your passions.

Passion is much like charisma. People have high charisma when they are passionate about what they're discussing. The second thing that brings charisma and influence is when there is commonality. This bonding of similarity brings about instant connection and passion! You should see me when I meet another nurse. I may not know them, but an instantaneous conversation between us could go on forever.

You can take the nurse out of the hospital, but you can't take the nurse out of the soul. There is a cliche that a nurse's passion is to help others become well, which is why they became a nurse. As a nurse of 18 years, it was rewarding to help others, yet that was not my reason for becoming a nurse. Interestingly, it was not typical for a patient to get better, which made me feel fulfilled. Instead, I cherished a patient's healing through the closure and finding their inner truth. Throughout my nursing career, I realized I felt most alive with passion while being with others, specifically in their darkest hour. I remember all the tears flowing, and I sat silently at the end of a bed. I listened, held a hand, and held the space. When I left these moments, I could feel myself walking on air, and being present was the best gift of healing I could give them. Looking back, I know I may have touched so many other lives, not knowing the power these interactions had. My heart grew so big inside me, knowing I was there in those moments with that person's soul as they moved through their pivotal experience. This soulful healing was part of the universe's magic.

I realize my passion also revolves around discussing the many facets of magic in the universe. "If you don't believe in magic, you will never find it." My younger sister told me these words had become my life's foundation. On this groundwork of believing in magic, I continue to learn more about the universe and shared consciousness. I find myself talking and often pausing, trying to assess where my listener is in their belief of magic. When I say magic, I mean the ability to think outside the box without the limitation of rules. When you believe in something with conviction, magic happens. Faith can move mountains, after all. But how often do we believe these so-called miracles are possible for us, not just others?

Planting a seed in someone's mind opens them up to the possibility of belief beyond what they thought existed—a seed of hope, a seed of maybe, a seed of what if. I love teaching that we all have a choice and can live any life we want. Getting to a place to believe and know this takes practice and patience. Yet, abundance, love, and joy are readily available and can flow into anyone. It is my passion to help others receive these birthrights.

I embraced guidance before seeing and receiving the gifts of abundance, love, and joy. During this guidance program, I was able to change myself. The magic was seeing everything around me change as well. After witnessing what was possible through firsthand experience, I was excited to share what I learned. A whole new way to support others was available to me. I was able to help patients, staff, strangers, and family members in a whole new way.

Life seems to have a new light when you feed your passion. Your perspective shifts from "life is happening to me" to "life is happening for me" and, ultimately, "life is happening because of me." Continuing my self-growth feeds my soul and makes life more vibrant. How much more can I grow when I practice giving up judgment, validation, and comparison? Reflecting on situations and removing the labeling of them as right, wrong, good, or bad is also life-changing. Seeing past challenges as blessings and teachings all in divine timing for my growth has been freeing. It truly is all about perspective. I have given myself forgiveness, which is often more challenging than forgiving others. We are often trapped in our painful thoughts that are emotionally charged. We can move forward only when we step out of our bodies and see what that pain is trying to show us. Pause to think of how you talk and treat yourself. Usually, we would never say the harmful things we say to ourselves to others. However, when we become our biggest supporters, put ourselves first, and acknowledge our worthiness, our world changes to reflect this. Our outer reality always mirrors our inner reality. This self-love will pour onto others, yet the key is first to fill our cup.

I read a book titled *Love Is the Solution* by Nasser Zaghi, and the concept presented there stayed with me. The book speaks to many world problems and acknowledges that the solution to each unique problem can be solved with love. If love is applied at the root of each problem, the problem ceases to exist. Love is the common denominator. Repeating this theme of the book countless times has wired it into my mind. I agree: love does solve everything. When debating how to solve the world's issues, I always come back to love. The person I am speaking with often says, "Well, not everyone is going to love each other." I simply respond, "BUT IF they did, then what?" I get the answer, "Well, there would be no issues."

I dream of bringing all children into this world to have a loving home. Children are open to magic. They have no reason to doubt that anything is possible. Doubt comes from what adults teach them. One of the most harmful words we can use for a child is "can't." Instantly, their hopes, dreams, faith, and magic are wiped away.

Spreading love and magic starts with me. I must create, offer, and inform the world that magic exists. In the words of TikTok, "Say it louder for those in the back." TikTok is also a passion of mine. I love how it makes "all" information accessible to the masses. It allows everyone to be creators and shine their light. I see all the encouraging support people give to each other. The algorithm truly helps you find the tribe that matches your vibe. I like to explain the power of TikTok as if I had an apple and I gave you an apple, then I no longer have an apple, but you have an apple. However, if I have an idea and give you one, we both have one. That is the magic, power, and strength of TikTok. Social media is here; how you choose to use it is up to you. I recognize that technology can be addicting, and its goal is to keep people scrolling. Still, I also enjoy having the opportunity to be exposed to new ideas and new people. Then if I choose to go deeper, I may. By its nature, TikTok nurtures creators to be vulnerable and real. I use TikTok to inspire me. Just remember to stop scrolling. You already have much knowledge to share and are ready to start creating!

I want to reach the nurses looking to be no longer stressed. I want to reach the nurses who want to help others using a blend of Western medicine and holistic and spiritual modalities. I have been away from the nursing field for two years. I want to tell them not to be afraid to choose differently and follow their passion. They are not bound by all the years of studying, all the debt, the blood, and the sweat equity they have put into their nursing career. I often hear, "This is all I can do," or "It is too late to do something else." I want to lead by example to show that this is not true. We create our reality; we must change our mindset and what we say to ourselves. Abundance will flow to us when we follow our passion.

Pharmaceutical companies often offer a wonderful dinner as they teach us about a new product or drug. I am familiar with attending these dinners to support my local oncology nursing society chapter. Since I encourage treating the root cause of a problem rather than using medication to mask the symptoms, it was magic to my ears when I heard about a unique dinner topic. Instead of a drug name that I could not pronounce in the title was one on caretaker burnout! I drove an hour away to attend this interactive dinner presentation focusing on compassion fatigue.

As the dinner progressed, I noticed I could not keep my hands from covering my eyes as I tried to eat dinner. Your body often makes noises or movements you are unaware of to express itself. This topic brought up everything inside of me from my recent nursing past. Every moment when I had a 12-hour shift and did not get a chance to use the restroom or take lunch, I could remember the feeling of dread as I had to watch my staff work while on the brink of tears. I looked around the room, and although people were participating since the discussion was encouraged, I could see that I was visibly more upset than the rest. I wondered why they were not fired up. After all, they have endured two years of a pandemic. That's when I realized they were still in the trenches. I've been out of the profession for two years and am still recovering from the trauma. It had taken me until now to slow down while making my food and enjoying my meals after 16 years of never knowing when I would get to eat or if my 30-minute lunch would be interrupted. Unfortunately, these nurses might not be aware of the damage this accumulating stress will lead to.

There is a new catchphrase in nursing: "self-care for healthcare." However, self-care does not work unless you do it. Just like reading a self-help book, the advice does not benefit the reader until that advice is applied. I want these nurses to know that they need to take action. If this means leaving the bedside, I hope to urge them to walk away and embrace what is best for them. One might even say unplugging from the matrix or stimulation. We all have a choice. It takes practice to see things as a choice and embrace the unknown—the unknown of a new path in life or perhaps modifying their current career.

I also love blending holistic healing with our current Western medicine. Emergency medicine, such as surgery for a broken leg, is terrific. Just as remarkable is clearing the root cause of chronic alignments. The body holds onto so many things energetically, and 40 years later, this trauma can manifest into disease. This is why it is important to practice letting go and forgiveness, especially when it comes to forgiving ourselves. When battling chronic alignment, there is time to remedy the situation and try other healing modalities. When I suggest a healing touch or a frequency-healing device, I tell people it is worth trying since it is non-invasive. I have seen so much healing from energy healing modalities. Healing comes in many forms. Yet these forms overlap and narrow down to the power of faith and intention. When you believe in something, that is what makes it powerful.

One can heal or harm itself by thought alone. Just as excitement and fear have the same reaction in the body, healing simply boils down to how one perceives it. I believe in the power of thoughts and words. Words are spells, and we must be careful what we say to others and ourselves. Thoughts have the power to change and even create our reality. Changing our thoughts ends with us. The collective still holds shared thoughts, and this collective consciousness controls some of our external reality.

I've discovered that I must balance my passion with sharing my belief in magic. Wanting others to embrace it before they are ready serves neither them nor me. I have felt the gift of letting go of the battles I cannot win. There is no reason to become frustrated if someone does not believe in magic. I let it go. I planted a seed, and if it chooses to grow, it will. If someone truly believes down to their subconscious in whatever form of healing, it will heal them. I wish for all to know that they are loved and have the power to choose their reality. I have come to understand that everything is in divine timing and alignment and to not judge the current situation as bad or good. I look back at all my challenges or life events and can only see their beauty now. When a soul comes to this life knowing that it is about to have all these amazing experiences unique to having a human body, it would never turn back. So, each experience is divine, and to refrain from viewing it as right or wrong is an acquired art form.

I never lacked passion. Passion is so simple that it's often overlooked and not considered passion. But passion doesn't need to be explained. It doesn't need to be elaborated on. It just is. Living means we experience passion, sometimes a longing for something more fulfilling. Today I start creating more to touch more people and inspire them. The best abundance comes from when you are living your passion. The next greatest abundance comes from helping others while doing your passion. The abundance in life increases with the number of others we reach. This chapter is a thank-you to the universe. My life is still changing, and I recognize that I am letting go of more of the known. I choose to remain in a state of embracing the unknown. The beautiful gifts waiting for me exceed the container of my imagination. This infinite, limitless world of possibilities is ready to grow your passions and move forward with trust. This was a knock on my door telling me to get started. As I end this chapter, I passionately continue the dance of my renewed journey.

"If passion drives you, let reason hold the reins."

~ Benjamin Franklin

CHAPTER ELEVEN

---∘◦∘◦∘---

Let Passion Guide You Through Life's Challenges

By John Spender

Section 1: What Does Passion Mean?

I pulled into the driveway for my third quote of the afternoon. The sun was shining bright; it was the height of summer, but I didn't feel so bright. It was just another late afternoon of quotes, and I felt frustrated and dead inside. This was my fifth year running my landscape gardening business, with abundant work and a balance of time off to travel to incredible locations globally.

However, deep down, I knew something was missing. I felt like every time I went traveling, I was escaping a career I no longer enjoyed. I was completely devoid of any passion for the work that once set me alight, jumping out of bed early in the morning. I was going through the motions instead of living with passion. I couldn't say it was bad; honestly, I was living a life that many clients and friends were envious of. However, I was finding it harder and harder to get up and get on with the usual cycle of things. Where did my drive go?

I began seeking and surfing the net for career and investment opportunities. Eventually, I came across a gentleman who ran a successful personal development company and was offering a free book before attending one of his four-day seminars. The book was *What I Wish I Had Learned at School But Didn't*. I loved the title. I felt the subject was one that most people could relate to after being trapped in the school system for over a decade. The book was about the author's journey to becoming a full-time investor; his discussion was 80% psychology and 20% investment strategies and counsel about legal and financial planning loopholes. I wasn't sure if investing was my next career move, but I was curious to learn how to manage my finances more deeply. The section on mindset was mind-blowing, and I was excited as I signed up for the author's yearly membership.

I then attended the author's four-day seminar. Each speaker at the event shared their life-changing epiphanies that led them to live a life of freedom. For them, every day was a holiday; the only difference was the vehicle they had chosen. The main speaker delivered the psychology part of the seminar, and he resonated passion with stories and demonstrations. I felt a broad spectrum of emotions, from excitement and doubt to curiosity and nervousness. I became energized as I tuned in to his every word. After that, I thought *I would sign up for whatever program he is offering.* Another abundantly clear thing was that the passion for my current vocation had well and truly died. Now it was time to develop a new passion and purpose.

So, what does passion mean?

> "When you catch a glimpse of your potential, that's
> when passion is born."
> ~ Zig Ziglar

I have learned that listening and acting on the heart's calling takes immense courage. So often, the very thing that will awaken our passion terrifies us and takes us out of the comfort zone that we get so good at creating. Yet, passion is a powerful, absorbing, and effective process, which can feel like "little destinies" calling from our unconscious or higher selves.

At first, these destinies take us on a mental journey where our mind is elsewhere, dreaming about the impact of these destinies. How could our lives be if we followed them? Yet, the destinies also function as mobilizers, energizers that get us out of bed and through challenging times.

One of the most exciting things about passions is their lack of logical order at dawn. Instead, they appear and stick there, lodged in a unique space in our minds. They can go unnoticed for days or even years, but those energizers are part of you.

No matter their name, the key is identifying, developing, cultivating, and collaborating with our passion. Why? To energize and bring meaning to our lives.

It's essential to take the time to reflect on what we truly love and what brings us joy. It could be diving, walking, drawing, playing football, reading, making a difference in our community, or other activities in any kind of charm. If it energizes you and does not negatively affect anyone else, go for it. For me, it's yoga, speaking, writing, traveling, and publishing books. So naturally, I didn't discover these things simultaneously; my passions have evolved.

My passion for traveling started when I was twenty-five. My then-girlfriend was from the Czech Republic, and I was curious about her country of birth. I asked her many questions about the culture, customs, and life during Russia's communist regime. We planned my first overseas trip to visit her family, including a stopover in Vienna. I was so excited. Months before we were due to fly out, I would ask colleagues and clients at the health club I worked at in St. Leonard's, Sydney, about their travel adventures. I felt like I was reliving their experiences. I was in awe, feeling energized and inspired by their tales. One common thread about all the travel escapades I heard was that they were one-off trips or too far from each other. I promised myself that if I caught the travel bug, I would find a way to travel overseas every year!

Of course, the trip was an epic holiday, and I loved the adventure, culture, and new places. Since that trip some twenty years ago, I have traveled overseas yearly. I continue to have incredible adventures around the world. This passion has evolved from pure holidays of activities and relaxation to more of a digital nomad life, working and living worldwide.

Passion is a fuel that can be "toxic" if one follows the pre-established order of society where there are routines, studies, and goals, all led by third parties to please them. The second fuel source is "renewable," and those energies are known as passions.

> "Passion is energy. Feel the power that comes from
> focusing on what excites you."
> ~ Oprah Winfrey

Discovering Your Passion

I've always been interested in the idea of finding my passion. I understood that the first step towards living a life driven by passion was discovering how to move from theory to action. Finding my passion was crucial to unlocking my potential and living a life full of meaning and purpose. I believe that passion can help us overcome challenges and obstacles. Remember the author and speaker I told you about? Well, I signed up for his year-long coaching program. After six months, I sold my landscaping business, became a full-time coach, and, three years later, moved that business from an office to online sessions over Skype. Living in Bali and traveling overseas every second month, I combined my passion for travel with my drive to help people find their passion and live with fulfillment. My coaching business eventually evolved into a boutique publishing house that I run to the present day.

I've learned a lot about living with passion over the years. Often, passion is mistaken for a "goal" in expressions such as "follow your passion." It also measures "intensity," such as "do it with passion." But how do I know if I am in front of a true passion? What defines a passion? I've realized there is a four-point consensus on what passions are.

How do I recognize a passion?

1. **Passions lead us to action**. Writing, public speaking, dancing, hiking, cooking, reading… Your passions drive you to action.

2. **Passions evolve.** Passion gives you the foundation. What you do with it is up to you. Think of your passion as if you were purchasing a smartphone. You can use only WhatsApp, Twitter, and YouTube with their basic set. Turning the phone into your little personal assistant is up to you. One of the fundamental characteristics of passions is that they set the foundations for our interests, which is why they can evolve. It's as if they were foundational classes: literature, science, and math. After acquiring knowledge in those areas, many application opportunities open.

3. **Passions are flexible**. As we change, we can shape our passions to fit our circumstances. *"When life gives you lemons, make lemonade."* A passionate cook can make creative and delicious dishes with the ingredients they have around them. They may have hundreds of options or fresh ingredients at home in every corner of their house, but if they must cook in a different place, they adapt. Their passion does not disappear but is likely reinvented. They never know what they might discover.

4. **Passions energize us**. No matter how exhausted we can be, passions are like that part of our stomach reserved for our favorite dessert. We are craving them.

How do I know it is not a passion?

5. **Passions are not careers.** They support careers. The reason for this slight change in perspective is self-explanatory. Career paths change, particularly with the advancement of society. However, their foundations remain the same, as do passions. There is no such thing as a "passion for engineering"; an engineer feels passion for the systems and processes that lead to building something, making them passionate about their career. Doctors do not have a "passion for medicine"; they feel passionate about diving into people's or animals' health. A writer does not have a "passion for writing"; they feel passionate about expressing messages in writing in the best possible way.

6. **Passions are not a place or thing.** Passions are not an end or goal but an engine to achieve them.

7. **Passions are not natural-born attributes.** We are not born with passions; we discover them. The more we are exposed to different cultures, environments, countries, activities, and books, the broader the spectrum of things that catch our attention. From this process, our passions arise.

8. **Passion is not an emotion.** Passion is often misunderstood as simply an emotion, but it's much more than that. While "passion" is commonly used to describe intense emotions or feelings, it's more accurate to describe passion as a driving force or impetus that propels a person towards their goals and aspirations. While emotions can undoubtedly be a part of passion, passion is more about the energy and momentum that comes from a heartfelt commitment to something. Various factors, such as personal values, a sense of purpose, or a desire for achievement, can fuel this commitment.

- To better understand the nature of passion, it's useful to think of it as an inner flame that burns brightly within a person, giving them the energy and motivation to pursue their dreams and goals. This flame can be sparked by various things, such as a deep interest in a particular subject or activity, a sense of purpose or mission, or a desire to impact the world positively.

Now for the exercise!

You may have a vague sense of your passions, but if you haven't spent much time thinking about them, they can be tricky to identify. I'm excited to give you some tips to help you discover your passions in life. I recommend you do this three-step exercise.

- List your interests by answering these questions: What do I enjoy doing? What gives me energy? What kinds of things make me feel alive and excited about life?

- Identify your true passions with the above features.

- Once you've identified the activities that bring out these emotions in yourself (and others), consider how they relate. For example, one thing that could bring out those feelings for you is teaching yoga classes at the local community center. Another option could be volunteering at an animal shelter or helping run fundraisers for local charities. All three scenarios are ways to give back while also enjoying yourself!

As a result, your list might be set up like this:

Interest	Passion	Emotion	Relate to
EcoFarming	Growing fresh vegetables	Fulfilled	Sustainability

Section 2: Cultivating Passion

Once you have discovered your passion, it's essential to cultivate and nurture it. This can be done in a few ways, including hiring a mentor, practicing regularly, and seeking opportunities for growth and development.

One way to cultivate your passion is to set achievable goals for yourself. These goals can be short-term or long-term but should be specific and measurable. For example, if your passion is painting, you might aim to complete one new painting each week. As you achieve your goals, you will feel a sense of accomplishment and motivation to continue pursuing your passion.

It's also helpful to practice regularly. Whether practicing a musical instrument, writing every day, or taking a class to learn new skills, consistent practice is essential to improving and growing your passion. This will help you build confidence and momentum, and you will begin to enjoy your passion even more as you improve.

Finally, seeking out opportunities for growth and development can help you cultivate your passion. This might include attending workshops, reading books, or joining a community of like-minded individuals who share your passion. In addition, exposing yourself to new ideas and perspectives can expand your knowledge and skills and keep your passion fresh and exciting.

Section 3: Know Your Values

As you consider the challenges that may come your way, it's important to remember that knowing your values can help guide your decisions. This is because values are deeply held beliefs about what is important in life, where you spend your money, and where you spend your time.

Your values are the guiding principles that help you make decisions and set priorities in your life. They often reflect your core beliefs about love but can also relate to other topics, such as family or contribution. They can help you identify what is important and align your actions with your goals and aspirations. For example, pursuing a passion that allows you to express yourself through art, music, or writing may be fulfilling if you value creativity and self-expression. Likewise, volunteering or participating in a social cause related to your passion could help you feel more connected and purposeful if you value community and making a positive impact.

You can ensure you live a meaningful and fulfilling life by aligning your passion with your values. Take some time to reflect on your values and how they relate to your passion. This can help you make more intentional choices about how to spend your time and energy.

Section 4: Living Your Best Life

You're the only one who can determine what brings you alive. It's not a question of whether you have passion but how much time and energy you put into pursuing it.

Living the fullest life possible means doing more of what excites you. This includes prioritizing and finding ways to incorporate your passions into your daily life. This doesn't necessarily mean quitting your job or making drastic changes, but it does mean being intentional with your time and energy. After all, we only live once—or at least we can live that way. This is true even if you believe in reincarnation. Experiences are unique, so there is no time to waste.

One way to live your best life is to make time for your passions. This could mean carving out time every day, every week, or every month to pursue your passion. It could also mean adjusting your schedule or routine to accommodate your passion. For example, if your passion is running, you might get up earlier in the morning to go for a run before work.

Another way to live your best life is to surround yourself with people who support and encourage your passion. This may mean joining a community of like-minded people who share your passion or simply talking to friends and family about your goals and aspirations.

Ultimately, living your best life means staying true to yourself and pursuing the things that matter to you. This way, you can find more fulfillment and happiness in your everyday life.

Section 5: The Power of Choice

One of the most important things to remember when facing challenges is that you always have a choice. Passions belong to the magical world of motivations, which gives them infinite power; however, in life's journey, you must adapt to the circumstances. Events can be seen from various perspectives; some are more positive than others, but that does not detract from their integrity. Therefore, only you know your passions and when to follow them. I recommend that you be mindful of the myths about passions since they often lead to a transcendental change in our lives.

Myths about passions

- **All passions are positive.** Not necessarily. For example, they can be counterproductive to your health or negatively impact others. Therefore, passions must be handled cautiously as a maxim in codes of conduct.

9. **If you don't do it regularly, it's not a genuine passion.**
   Your passions are buried within you, and you need to discover them. They are natural yearnings; you may find them early on in life and then lose touch with them. A genuine passion for something is like riding a bike; no matter how long it's been, when you return, it feels like you've never ceased knowing how to ride it. Passions always remain in your memories because of the reaction, which is often visceral. You may not practice them, but like everyone else, you may find the right moment to pursue them. This does not detract from the veracity of your passion.

"There is no passion for being found playing small—in settling for a life that is less than the one you are capable of living."
~ Nelson Mandela

- **You are driven by one passion.** Good news: the passion plan you are born with is unlimited. The key thing is to identify two points: whether the passions are things you can enjoy and what you can do with them. For example, someone passionate about mathematics could become an engineer, an accountant, or a teacher. On the other hand, she could keep the family business accounts or her passion to herself and do nothing with it. Ironically, doing nothing is the most popular alternative. Once again, you have the power to decide.

  You can choose to do what you love, or you can choose not to. The first option will lead you toward fulfillment and happiness; the second will leave you feeling unfulfilled and unhappy.

  It might sound obvious, but it's important because it not only reminds us that we always have options but also helps us realize how powerful our decisions are in shaping our lives—and how much potential there is for change if we make different choices!

Section 6: Let Passion Pull You Through Challenges

Life is full of challenges, and it's easy to feel overwhelmed and lost in adversity. But one thing that can help guide you through these difficult times is your passions. Having something you truly care about can give you the strength and motivation to push through even the toughest obstacles.

Passions are powerful drivers that help you stay focused, motivated, and energized. When you are passionate about something, you have a deep emotional connection to it, and it becomes a source of purpose and meaning in your life. Whether it's a hobby, a career, or a personal goal, your passions can help you stay connected to your values and priorities, giving you the resilience and determination to keep moving forward.

But passion is not just about feeling good; it's also about doing good. Pursuing your passions makes you more likely to be engaged, creative, and productive. Passionate people are often the ones who make a positive impact in their communities and the world. This is because they have a sense of purpose and direction that helps them channel their energy and talents toward making a difference.

So, how can you let your passions pull you through life's challenges? Here are some tips:

- **Stay tuned to your passions.** It's easy to lose sight of your passions during a difficult time. But it's important to keep them in mind and stay connected to them. Make time for the things you love, even just a few minutes daily. Surround yourself with people who share your passions and support your goals.

- **Use your passions as a source of motivation**. When facing a tough challenge, consider how your passions can help you overcome it. Use your passion as a source of inspiration and motivation. Imagine how achieving your goals will make you feel, and use that feeling to fuel your determination.

- **Stay open to new opportunities.** Your passions can guide you toward new opportunities and experiences. So, stay open to new ideas and possibilities, and be willing to take risks and try new things. You always need to find out where your passions might lead you!

- **Feel free to ask for help or support.** Sometimes, even the most passionate and driven people need help. So, don't be afraid to reach out to others for support and guidance. Whether it's a mentor, a friend, or a professional, some people can help you navigate your challenges.

Your passions can be a powerful tool for navigating life's challenges. By staying connected to your passions, using them as a source of motivation, staying open to new opportunities, and asking for help when needed, you can harness the power of your passions to overcome even the most formidable obstacles.

"Chase down your passion like it's the last bus of the night."

~ Terri Guillemets

Author Biographies

Julie Blouin

CHAPTER ONE

Julie Blouin is a Certified Professional Coach and a leading voice in the personal development industry with over 20 years of experience. Her passion for coaching started at the age of six when she began coaching her Cabbage Patch Kids in her own "School of Life." Julie is a 3-time International Bestselling Co-Author and has written over 100 articles about career, health, and relationships.

As a widely recognized expert in empowerment, mindset, gratitude, and business coaching, Julie has facilitated coaching courses and corporate training for hundreds of employees in organizations featured in Canada's Top 100 Employers. Her contributions have been recognized in various media outlets, including TV, radio, podcasts, magazines, newspapers, and summits. Julie enjoys traveling the world, is fluent in English and French, and speaks intermediate Spanish. Her magnetic and radiant presence as a motivational speaker has made her a popular choice.

With her unique blend of personal experience, professional expertise, and motivational speaking, Julie Blouin is a powerful force in personal development, leadership, and peak performance. Through her books, events, coaching courses, and social media,

Julie has helped thousands worldwide take action, overcome their fears and limitations, and create the life they truly desire.

If you want to take your personal or professional life to new heights, reach out to Julie through her website at https://www.julieblouin.com or email her at julie@julieblouin.com to learn more about how she can help you and your organization.

Victoria Finch
CHAPTER TWO

Victoria Finch, "The Heart Healer, "is an Award-Winning Speaker, Author, and Success Coach. She also owns Avalon Virtual Assistants LLC, a top virtual assistant company.

She guides heart-centered coaches, speakers, and entrepreneurs from stuck to stellar by helping you rapidly release fear, anxiety, and limiting beliefs.

Victoria is a master at transforming and empowering others through her storytelling, books, speaking, workshops, and master classes.

Victoria is Certified as a Master Hypnotherapist and Master Practitioner of Emotional Freedom Techniques by the International Board of Coaches and Practitioners and The Complementary Therapists Accredited Association. She is also a Certified Cognitive Behavior Life Coach Practitioner.

Victoria has been in some dark places in her life. She never felt loved or wanted despite growing up in a loving home. She carried that feeling throughout her life. Even though she excelled at her studies and won awards, she never felt good enough.

Victoria went on a quest for self-acceptance and cracked the code to self-love and self-forgiveness. Her signature coaching programs are designed to guide heart-centered coaches, speakers, and entrepreneurs from stuck to stellar by helping rapidly release fear, anxiety, and limiting beliefs.

Victoria knows her purpose on earth is to heal the hearts of others that had accepted rejection as normal, just as she had done.

Holly Fair
CHAPTER THREE

Holly Fair, M.B.A. – Life Coach – Motivational Speaker – Ambassador of Royalty.

Holly lives a beautiful Queen life, but it wasn't always glorious. Holly's past is filled with profound traumas, including sexual, verbal, and physical abuse, losing a baby, infertility, and extreme weight fluctuations. However, these experiences gifted Holly with intense empathy, allowing her to connect with anyone deeply emotionally. So rather than becoming bitter toward life, she discovered the gifts the darkness held.

Holly discovered her true identity in a momentous breakthrough – that of a Queen! What began as a novelty of wearing a crown for photo ops has become a passion. She started her #CrownDayEveryDay challenge in October 2021 and has worn her crown every day since then, giving her a unique opportunity to show up, inspire others, and have meaningful conversations with people around the globe. Holly has become the self-proclaimed Ambassador for the royalty that lives within us all!

Holly honed her skills as a business professor for 13 years, delighting adult learners with her zest for teaching and empowering them to be the best they could be. A dynamic speaker, she inspires and captivates live and virtual audiences of all sizes. Now retired from her professorship, she teaches others how to rise above their limitations and create a life of meaning and impact.

Holly is pursuing her Doctorate in Holistic Life Coaching. She lives in Utah with her husband, Jamie, and tiny Papillon, Lola. She enjoys traveling and serving as a Senior Leader in the Tony Robbins organization in her free time.

Connect with Queen Holly Fair at http://www.facebook.com/QueenHollyFair
http://www.instagram.com/QueenHollyFair
holly@fireuplife.com

Debbie McKenzie
CHAPTER FOUR

Debbie McKenzie is a Multidimensional Energy Healer, Soul Alignment guide, Divine Blueprint Illuminator, author, and oracle deck creator. She has formal psychosynthesis coaching, nursing, Social Work, and counselling qualifications. Her thirty-year journey of self-growth has enabled her to support, mentor, uplift, and witness the transformation of others. She accomplishes this by combining the power of energy healing to transmute their limiting core beliefs, ignite their unique gifts and talents in their Divine Blueprint, and connect them to their 'I AM' presence to heal, evolve and shine their essence.

Her mission is to be a catalyst and uplifter in service to those who feel called to understand themselves more fully and the truth of whom they are by leading them deep into their core self of love, so they can activate their creative expression and intuition, reclaim their sovereign power and live from a space of loving kindness, conscious choice and inspired action in service to their life, their relationships and fulfillment of their unique role in this world.

This is Debbie's second book collaboration with Writer John Spender in his number one best-selling series, *A Journey of Riches*. Debbie's previous chapter was featured in *The Power of Inspiration*: *Twelve Stories to Spark Your Soul.*

Debbie is the creator of the *Heal, Evolve, Shine,* oracle deck with a guidebook to support people in cultivating their growth and expansion, and it is available via www.deckible.com.start

Debbie can be contacted via her website at healevolveshine.com or by email at healevolveshine@gmail.com.

Anthony Dierickx
CHAPTER FIVE

Anthony Dierickx experienced bullying at the age of five–six years old and, later in life, went through the ordeal of his parents' divorce at ten years old. These traumatic memories led him on the road of discovery in the self-development industry. As serendipity would have it, he was coached by some of the best coaches in this industry through their various materials – the most known are Anthony Robbins, Robert Kiyosaki, John Assaraf, and Dr. John Demartini. Career-wise, he completed his marketing degree at the University of South Australia in 2013 and graduated on August 19th, 2014.

He has travelled and explored different parts of the world, from the Great Wall of China, the Eiffel Tower in Paris, Batu Caves in Kuala Lumpur, the Islands of Fiji, Scuba Diving around Langkawi, Malaysia, Shark Cage Diving in Port Lincoln, South Australia, kayaking with the migrating Humpback Whales in Byron Bay New South Wales, Horse Riding in the Daintree Forest Queensland, and more while spreading words of unconditional love, connection, and community.

His proactive experience and Christian faith have guided others to live their optimum lifestyle. He has achieved this by coaching them to break free of their inner chains or battles, live in flow with their authentic selves, and ultimately be aligned with their true purpose!

He lives by his grandma's words of legacy left behind when she passed on Friday, 27th of November 2020 – "Le dernier mot revient a celui qui n'abandonne jamais," meaning "The last word remains with the one that never gives up!"

His mission statement – "To give a voice to the voiceless!"

He leaves a prayer for whoever reads this that God blesses you in every which way because this bio is not to impress upon you what achievements he has made but to emphasize that if he can do it, you can do it! God bless you.

Email: anthony.dierickx@gmail.com
Facebook - facebook.com/anthony.dierickx
LinkedIn - linkedin.com/in/anthony-d-57773731

Annette Korolenko
CHAPTER SIX

Annette is an Author and Life Coach.

Annette poetically orchestrates the essence of thoughts into words describing every heartfelt feeling.

Her book *Believe in Signs, Synchronicities, and Miracles* is almost completed.

From working as an interpreter for U.S. Press abroad, searching for meaning, to her passion and love of storytelling /writing/ screenwriting, she hopes to inspire.

She is the creator of Love Notes / Love Cards.

She has published articles and poetry in five international magazines. Books in progress:

Believe in Signs, Synchronicities, and Miracles
Journey of Women
Gypsy Stories
Adventures of Zip-Zap and Zoom-Zoom (children's stories)

She is also an International Best-Selling Author of *Messages From the Heart*.

To connect, email Annette at:
akblessed@yahoo.com. Tel. 224-500-8429

Inarra Aryane Griffyn

CHAPTER SEVEN

Inarra Aryane Griffyn is a Visionary Business Guide offering a Spiritual Elixir to creatives and entrepreneurs to help them gain expression, visibility, and opportunity. She helps stimulate and enhance her client's vision so that they generate, manifest, and experience luxury at their pace and in perfect timing.

To do this, using the ancient cycles of the seasons, Moon, and Solar alignments, such as the Spring Equinox or Autumn Equinox, she helps them activate new cycles of transformation. Her clients follow a series of mastery prompts, based on perfect timing to launch their products, programs, and projects. Her recipe of mastery skills helps them unfold into their next level of business and life. They experience quantum transformation by following her "Luxury in Harmony with Nature" recipe, and she has guided many high-level business owners to reach their dream life.

She teaches 11 Queens and 11 Kings Mastery Programmes online in London, UK. She also hosts retreats such as The Mysteries of Avalon in Glastonbury, UK. In addition, Inarra is a public speaker and author of four books, the latest being *The Little Book Of Influence,* published in 2021. *A High Priestess of Avalon,* she teaches ritual and the *Priestess Path*.

You can contact her directly by email at inarra@thevisionaries. international and on her social media platforms FB & Insta @ inarraaryanegriffyn @newearthvisionaries

To find out about her programs and coaching, join her mailing list and receive a free ebook https://optin.thevisionaries.international/ newearthvisionaries

Brandon Bates
CHAPTER EIGHT

Brandon lives a dedicated life to being the change we want to see. He's not big on complaining but loves game planning. From Cleveland to Phoenix, He wants this. He's sincere. He was able to create residual income and then was allowed to follow his dream to the "T."

In eight years, he figured out the laws of the universe that apply to all things moving, how to grow fruit and vegetables/herbs, how to manage a budget comparable to a single mom of 2-3 children, how to communicate effectively with all walks of life, how not to disregard folks just because they don't fit the immediate mold that is in place for most of us, and learn how to broker business deals all through sheer networking with a "love first" mindset.

He thanks his environment for giving him the character and pushing his love and desire for his passion.

Patrick Richard Garcia
CHAPTER NINE

Patrick Richard Garcia is a speech impairment & professional life coach, business consultant, and owner of Hustle Revival Enterprises. He helps male entrepreneurs and business owners to revive their hustle instincts through result-producing and intensive self-development activities simultaneously by mastering the art of communication.

Patrick is an Amazon best-selling author as a contributor to *Our Yellow Brick Road: An Anthology of Humans Who Believe in the Impact of Storytelling* - a compilation of 12 essays/stories that exemplify storytelling and celebrating community.

He is also an inspirational speaker, starting his first on-stage appearance on June 2017 at Speaker Slam: So You Think You Can Speak? Thereon, he started his journey of further developing his craft in storytelling and competing in competitions on and offline. He shared his powerful story regarding his learning disability and the adversity involved in being present where he is today.

Your Success Magazine recognized Patrick for his extraordinary commitment to the business, entrepreneurship, and personal development.

He currently resides in Toronto, ON, Canada.

Anne Henning
CHAPTER TEN

Anne Henning graduated with a Masters's degree in Spiritual Psychology. In 2018 she co-founded *I Choose Soul*, a platform that spreads an abundance mindset through spiritual-based techniques. Anne's greatest gift is the ability to nurture and support those on their spiritual journey.

A 15-year-long oncology nursing career shaped Anne's desire to treat the whole person, beyond the body, to include the mind and spirit. During her career, she became a supervisor and assisted the integrative therapy team in introducing holistic therapy in the hospital setting. In addition, Anne expanded a multifaceted self-care program to all healthcare personnel as the Nurse Practice Council Chair.

In response to the recent mass exodus of nurses and work-related fatigue, Anne developed a restorative retreat designed for nurses to replenish the whole self. The retreat blueprint exposes participants to a vast range of healing modalities. As a result, nurses are assisted with a transformation that brings them from burnout to creating a vibrant life full of joy.

Anne inspires people to live their best lives by living her life to the fullest. Her greatest bliss is working alongside her mother to promote a medical device they invented together. This simple device, the Beata Clasp, eases the nurse's daily frustration with tangled tubing. This is a legacy her mother is proud to leave behind, and Anne hopes she, too, can leave a lasting spiritual legacy in the lives of many nurses.

www.ichoosesoul.com

John Spender
CHAPTER ELEVEN

John Spender is a 31-time International Best-Selling co-author who didn't learn how to read and write at a basic level until he was ten. He has since traveled to more than 68 countries and territories and started many businesses leading him to create the best-selling book series *A Journey Of Riches*. In addition, he is an Award-Winning International Speaker and Movie Maker.

John worked as an international NLP trainer and coached thousands of people from various backgrounds through many challenges. From the borderline homeless to wealthy individuals, he has helped many people connect with their truth to create a life on their terms.

John's search for answers to living a fulfilling life has taken him to work with Native Americans in the Hills of San Diego, to the forests of Madagascar, swimming with humpback whales in Tonga, exploring the Okavango Delta of Botswana and climbing the Great Wall of China. He's traveled from Chile to Slovakia, Hungary to the Solomon Islands, the mountains of Italy, and the streets of Mexico.

Everywhere his journey has taken him, John has discovered a hunger among people to find a new way to live, with a yearning for freedom of expression. His belief that everyone has a book in them was born.

He is now a writing coach, having worked with over 400 authors from 40 countries for the *A Journey of Riches* series http://ajourneyofriches. com/ and his publishing house, Motion Media International, has published 32 non-fiction titles to date.

John also co-wrote and produced the movie documentary *Adversity* starring Jack Canfield, Rev. Micheal Bernard Beckwith, Dr. John Demartini, and many more, coming soon in 2022. And you can bet there will be a best-selling book to follow!

Afterword

I hope you enjoyed the shared heartfelt stories, wisdom, and vulnerability. Storytelling is the oldest form of communication, and I hope you feel inspired to take a step toward living a fulfilling life. Feel free to contact any of the authors in this book or the other books in this series.

The proceeds of this book will be used for social giving at Jewel Children's Home in North East Bali.

Other books in the series are…

Master Your Mindset: A Journey of Riches, Book Thirty-one
https://mybook.to/MasterYourMindset

Transform Your Wounds into Wisdom: A Journey of Riches, Book Thirty
https://www.amazon.com/dp/
B0BKTJ377N?th=1&psc=1&geniuslink=true

Motivate Your Life: A Journey of Riches, Book Twenty-Nine
https://www.amazon.com/dp/B0BCXMF11P

Awaken to Your Inner Truth: A Journey of Riches, Book Twenty-Eight
https://www.amazon.com/dp/B09YLYMQ4H?geniuslink=true

Awaken to Your Inner Truth: A Journey of Riches, Book Twenty-Eight
https://www.amazon.com/dp/B09YLYMQ4H?geniuslink=true

The Power of Inspiration: A Journey of Riches, Book Twenty-Seven
http://mybook.to/ThePowerofInspiration

Messages from The Heart: A Journey of Riches, Book Twenty-Six
http://mybook.to/MessagesOfHeart

Abundant Living: A Journey of Riches, Book Twenty-Five
https://www.amazon.com/dp/B0963N6B2C

The Way of the Leader: A Journey of Riches, Book Twenty-Four
https://www.amazon.com/dp/1925919285

The Attitude of Gratitude: *A Journey of Riches,* Book Twenty-Three
https://www.amazon.com/dp/1925919269

Facing Your Fears: *A Journey of Riches,* Book Twenty-Two
https://www.amazon.com/dp/1925919218

Returning to Love: *A Journey of Riches,* Book Twenty-One
https://www.amazon.com/dp/B08C54M2RB

Develop Inner Strength: *A Journey of Riches,* Book Twenty
https://www.amazon.com/dp/1925919153

Building your Dreams: A Journey of Riches, Book Nineteen
https://www.amazon.com/dp/B081KZCN5R

Liberate your Struggles: A Journey of Riches, Book Eighteen
https://www.amazon.com/dp/1925919099

In Search of Happiness: A Journey of Riches, Book Seventeen
https://www.amazon.com/dp/B07R8HMP3K

Tapping into Courage: A Journey of Riches, Book Sixteen
https://www.amazon.com/dp/B07NDCY1KY

The Power Healing: A Journey of Riches, Book Fifteen
https://www.amazon.com/dp/B07LGRJQ2S

The Way of the Entrepreneur: A Journey Of Riches, Book Fourteen
https://www.amazon.com/dp/B07KNHYR8V

Discovering Love and Gratitude: A Journey Of Riches, Book Thirteen
https://www.amazon.com/dp/B07H23Q6D1

Transformational Change: A Journey Of Riches, Book Twelve
https://www.amazon.com/dp/B07FYHMQRS

Finding Inspiration: A Journey Of Riches, Book Eleven
https://www.amazon.com/dp/B07F1LS1ZW

Building your Life from Rock Bottom: A Journey Of Riches, Book Ten
https://www.amazon.com/dp/B07CZK155Z

Transformation Calling: A Journey Of Riches, Book Nine
https://www.amazon.com/dp/B07BWQY9FB

Letting Go and Embracing the New: A Journey Of Riches, Book Eight
https://www.amazon.com/dp/B079ZKT2C2

Making Empowering Choices: A Journey Of Riches, Book Seven
https://www.amazon.com/Making-Empowering-Choices-Journey-Riches-ebook/dp/B078JXMK5V

The Benefit of Challenge: A Journey Of Riches, Book Six
https://www.amazon.com/dp/B0778S2VBD

Personal Changes: A Journey Of Riches, Book Five
https://www.amazon.com/dp/B075WCQM4N

Dealing with Changes in Life: A Journey Of Riches, Book Four
https://www.amazon.com/dp/B0716RDKK7

Making Changes: A Journey Of Riches, Book Three
https://www.amazon.com/dp/B01MYWNI5A

The Gift In Challenge: A Journey Of Riches, Book Two
https://www.amazon.com/dp/B01GBEML4G

From Darkness into the Light: A Journey Of Riches, Book One
https://www.amazon.com/dp/B018QMPHJW

Thank you to all the authors who have shared aspects of their lives, hoping to inspire others to live a bigger version of themselves.

Afterword

I want to share a beautiful quote from Jim Rohan, "You can't complain and feel grateful at the same time." At any given moment, we have a choice to either feel like a victim of life or be connected and grateful for it. I hope this book helps you feel grateful and inspires you to go after your dreams.

For more information about contributing to the series, visit http://ajourneyofriches.com/. Furthermore, if you enjoyed reading this book, we would appreciate your review on Amazon to help get our message out to even more readers.